MĀUI'S TAONGA TALES

MĀUI'S TAONGA TALES

A treasury of stories from Aotearoa and the Pacific

BASED ON THE TV SERIES HE PAKI TAONGA I A MĀUI

TE PAPA

PRESS

CONTENTS

HE KUPU WHAKATAKI

INTRODUCTION

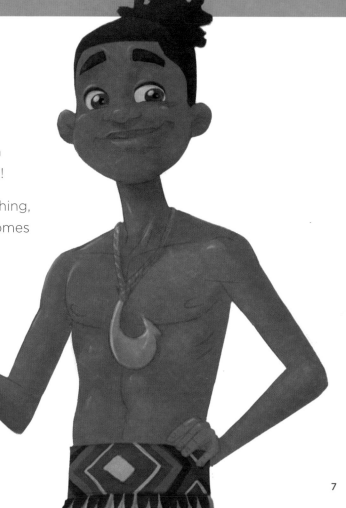

Kia ora e hoa mā,

You know me – Māui, famous explorer (and troublemaker!) all around Te Moana-nui-a-Kiwa, and right here in Aotearoa.

After a hard day slowing down the sun and stuff like that, I like to relax with a good story. I've put a bunch of my favourites in this pukapuka – lucky you!

These stories spring from amazing taonga. Meet a volcanic rock, and next thing, you're zooming with taniwha to rescue a frozen tohunga. From a kōauau comes the tale of a lovesick princess who went on a crazy adventure. There's even the actual kaitaka that saved a boy's life!

I've stuck in a story about me too – yeah, I know, I'm a show-off. I'll tell you the one about the magical matau that helped me snag Te Ika-a-Māui, the North Island.

So whai mai – let's go explore!

Ko Tāne me ngā Kete o te Wānanga

Tāne and the Kete of Knowledge

Kete whakairo

Take a look at the weaving on this kete from long ago.
It's beautiful. What would you put in a precious kete?
Could you carry ... knowledge? Sounds weird, but Tāne did.

STORY RETOLD BY VICTORIA CLEAL

ARTWORK BY MUNRO TE WHATA

Back then on Earth, there were only atua – no humans like us. Way at the top of the heavens, there was Io, the Great Spirit. One day, he invited Tāne up and gave him three baskets of knowledge, so everyone on Earth would have wisdom.

This invitation was a big deal, and Tāne's brother Whiro was super jealous.

'I'm as good as him!' he thought. 'I'll go a secret way and beat him to it.'

He started clambering up the sides of the first heaven. Good luck, Whiro – there's eleven more to go!

Tāne and his mates called on the wind children for help, and – whoosh – they were lifted straight to the third heaven.

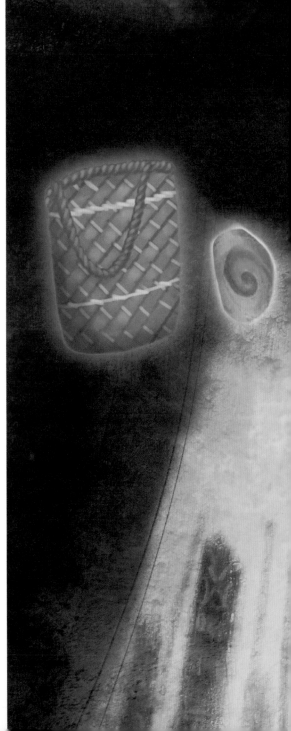

Whiro saw they were overtaking him, so he sent a terrifying weapon ... bugs. Zap! Hundreds of sandflies bit Tāne. Slurp! Swarms of waeroa sucked his friends' blood.

But Tāne and his friends called out, 'Children of the wind, blow them away!' and the bugs scattered.

Tāne travelled right up to the twelfth heaven – the house of Io. There, the Great Spirit told him, 'Tāne, I give you three precious baskets, carrying knowledge:

'**Aronui** – knowledge of peace and the arts,

'**Tuauri** – ancient knowledge of rituals and nature,

'and **Tuatea** – knowledge of technology, war, and sorcery.

'I also give you two whatukura – stones that hold the power of knowledge.'

Tāne began his journey back to Earth. But bugs swarmed at him – ten times more than before. Kāhu, kārearea and ruru swooped, pecking and tearing.

Then, Whiro sprang up and lunged at his brother. But Tāne was strong from the mana of the kete – he pushed Whiro aside.

The wind children blew the bugs and birds to Earth. They still live around you today.

As Tāne and his hoa came home, the sunset turned deep red with joy. Pūtātara blasted.

Tāne placed the kete and whatukura in the wharekura he'd built. The gifts brought wisdom to the atua – and to humans.

If you're learning a waiata or a haka, or if you're weaving, you're dipping into a basket of knowledge. See the poutama pattern? Those are the steps to learning – they remind us of Tāne's epic journey.

Luckily, these days, you don't have to trek to heaven to know stuff!

Ko te Kaitaka Whakaora o Ruhia

Ruhia's Life-saving Cloak

Kaitaka

This cloak is pretty special – it saved a boy's life! It belonged to Ruhia Pōrutu. She had heaps of mana, and her father-in-law, Te Rīrā Pōrutu, was a chief of Pipitea pā in Wellington.

Ruhia had no idea that one day her beautiful cloak would be the only thing standing between Te Rīrā and the life of a young boy fresh off the boat from England.

STORY RETOLD BY MATTHEW GRAINGER WITH THE KIND SUPPORT OF TE ĀTI AWA AND NGĀTI HĀMUA/TE MATEHOU
ARTWORK BY ARIKI BRIGHTWELL

This all happened in 1840, in Pōneke – some people call it Wellington these days. Pōneke was a great port where settlers arrived to make a new home in Aotearoa.

One of them was Thomas McKenzie. He was just twelve years old and he had arrived on a ship called the *Adelaide*. He was alone in a strange place, with nowhere to go.

'Better find somewhere to sleep,' he said to his friend Edwin, who'd arrived with him.

In the dead of night, Thomas and Edwin found themselves on the green hillsides of Pipitea, where a great house was being built. It was empty and the door was open. 'The perfect place to sleep,' thought Thomas.

Thomas didn't know that to sleep in an unfinished house is tapu. He didn't know that the punishment for breaking tapu was death!

Chief Te Rīrā and his people were building the house. Te Rīrā and thirty of his iwi, including Ruhia, came to check on it. They discovered the two boys asleep in the house and confronted them.

Te Rīrā's haka was fierce and his mere pounamu flashed in the dark.
The boys were terrified – Te Rīrā looked like he wanted to kill them.

But Ruhia saw both sides. The boys didn't know that the house was tapu or that they'd done anything wrong.

Just as Te Rīrā was about to teach them a lesson, Ruhia threw her cloak over the boys.

Yep, nobody was killed that night. Because throwing a cloak over someone the way Ruhia did gives protection from harm. Thomas and Edwin were saved.

But that's not all ...

Thomas remained a lifelong friend of Ruhia and her family. And when Thomas died, the kaitaka was placed over his casket at his funeral – the taonga that had saved his life protected him in death, too. Cool story, eh?

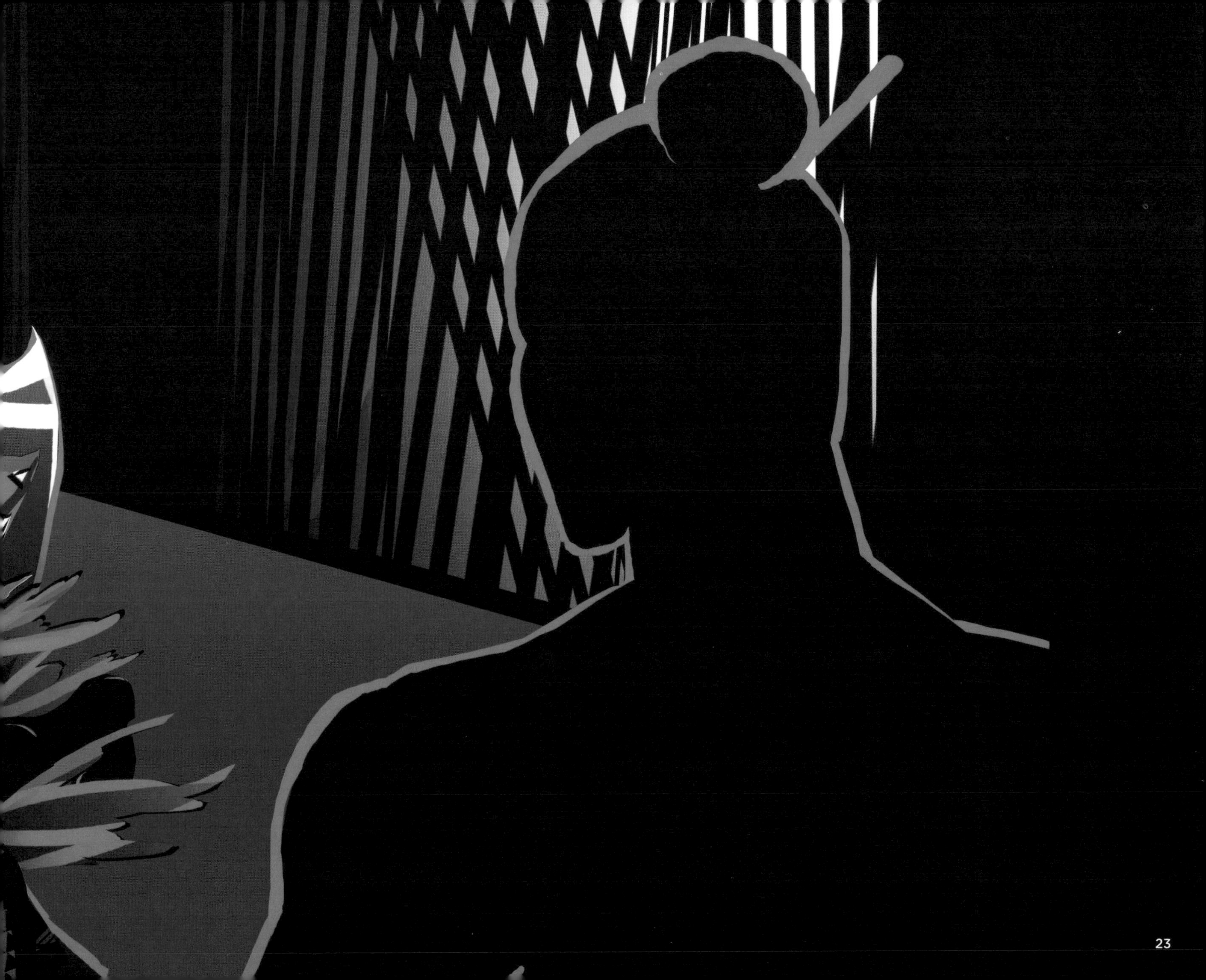

Te Tūtakinga Kino o te tau 1769

The Deadly Encounter of 1769

Hoe

This is a hoe, a paddle, stained red with kōkōwai and painted with pītau patterns in a style called kōwhaiwhai.

In 1769, this hoe right here was traded by Māori with crew members on board a sailing ship called the *Endeavour*. You might have heard of the ship's captain: James Cook. He's who Cook Strait is named after. When he came to Aotearoa for the first time, things between Māori and his crew didn't get off to a good start.

STORY RETOLD BY MATTHEW GRAINGER WITH THE KIND SUPPORT OF RONGOWHAKAATA IWI TRUST
ARTWORK BY MUNRO TE WHATA

The great tohunga, Te Toiroa, of Mahia, predicted they would come – red and white strangers. And three years later, a ship appeared on the horizon off the coast of Tūranga-nui-a-Kiwa.

Some unusual-looking men came ashore. They were Europeans.

Te Maro, of Ngāti Oneone, came towards them to perform a wero.

A European fired a warning shot. Te Maro knew nothing of guns and continued his wero. Another shot and Te Maro lay dead.

The next morning, on the bank of the Tūranganui, a group of local men watched as more Europeans rowed toward the shore. The local men began a mighty haka.

The sound of a musket rang out. Stunned, the men waited to see what would happen next.

A voice among the Europeans called out in a familiar language. It was Tūpaia, a chief from Tahiti who was travelling with Cook. He told them that all they wanted was food and water.

So some of the men swam out to the great rock, Te Toka-a-Taiau. Among them was Te Rākau of Rongowhakaata. There, they met Cook. Their hongi was the first time Māori and European formally greeted one another.

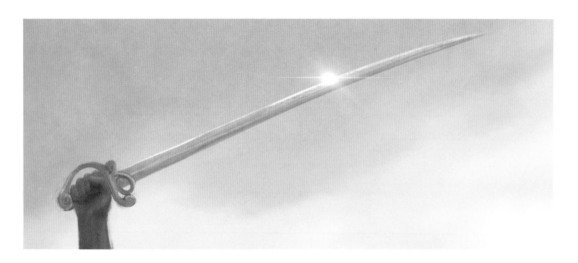

But the peace didn't last. Te Rākau snatched a sword from one of Cook's men – and was shot and killed. Three more men were killed soon after.

Later, Cook's men tried to force some men out fishing to talk. When the men paddled away, the Europeans shot at them. The men threw stones and hoe and fish at the Europeans, who fired again. Two men were killed on the spot, and two others were mortally wounded.

Cook and his men soon sailed away. They had taken the lives of nine Tūranga people. Cook took the name of their bay, too. He called it Poverty Bay. But its real name is Tūranga-nui-a-Kiwa.

It had been a terrible and deadly first meeting. Misunderstanding had led to great tragedy. This hoe, this taonga, was there – and it reminds us of what can happen when people choose to fight before they try to understand.

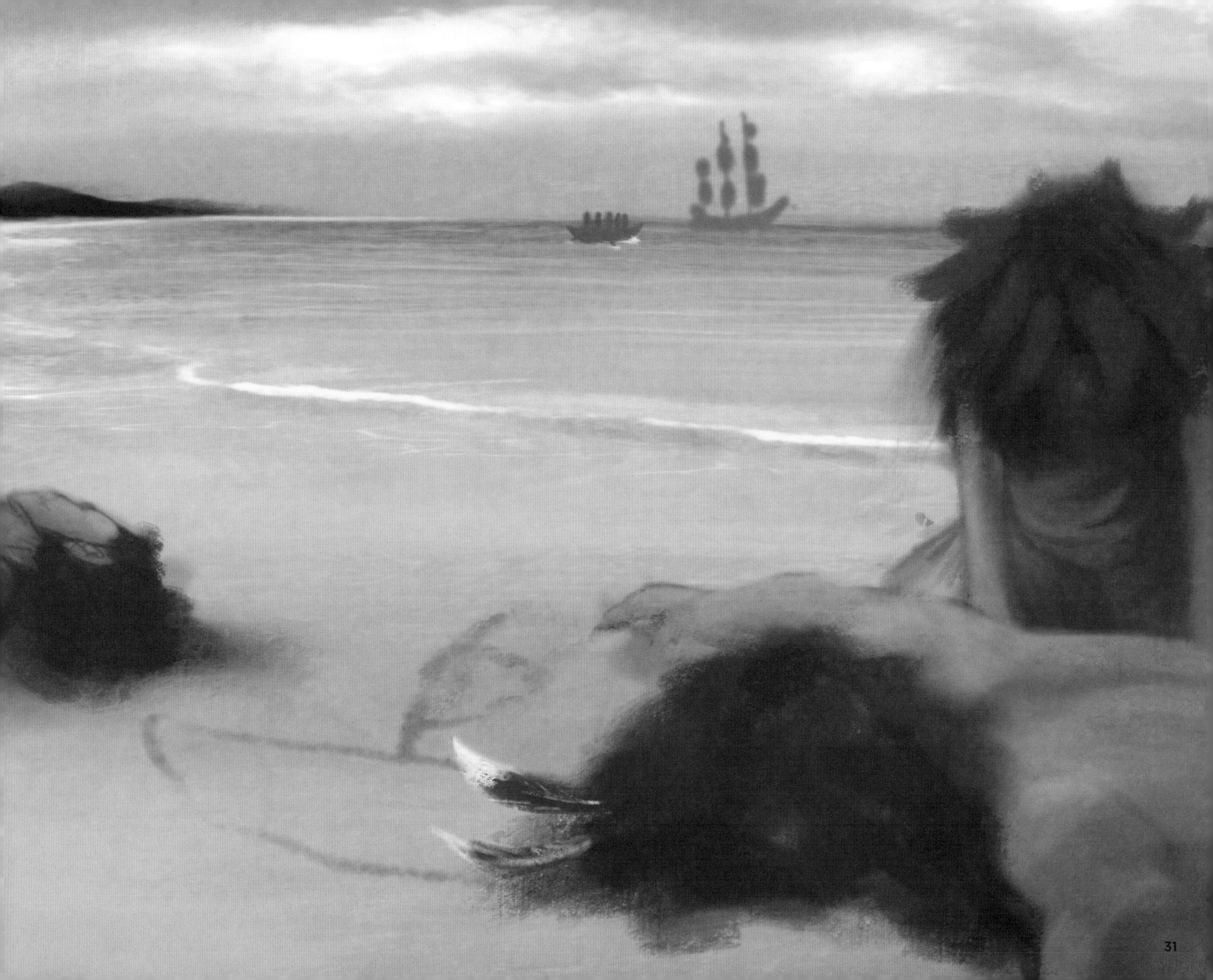

Ko te Pakanga a ngā Manu

Battle of the Birds

Kahu huruhuru

Come closer – check out this stunning kahu huruhuru. See the feathers woven together? Thousands of them! They're from kākā, tūī, kererū ... Yeah, I know them all. I even turned into a kererū once.

It's peaceful in the bush now, but once, those manu got caught up in a mean battle. Not their fault – two kawau started it.

STORY RETOLD BY VICTORIA CLEAL
ARTWORK BY ISOBEL JOY TE AHO-WHITE

One day, Sea Kawau ran into his
cousin, Land Kawau. 'Come over to
my place!' he said. 'I've got the best
fishing spot in the world.'

'Yeah, right,' Land Kawau said.
'I mean – yeah, I'm sure you're right.'

At Sea Kawau's fishing ground, they dived again and again – but there wasn't one ika. Sea Kawau puffed with rage – how dare the fish make him look stupid!

'No biggie,' Land Kawau said. 'Maybe we can scratch up something at my humble little awa.'

Turned out his river was bursting
with juicy tuna. But Sea Kawau was
getting all hot inside – like when you
see your cousin's new trainers, and
they've got lights on top and neon
shoelaces. 'Not fair!' he thought.

By the time he got home, he was boiling. He rounded up all the seabirds. 'Those land birds,' he said, 'they've got better kai. We should attack them!' The birds squawked in agreement.

Only Tītī shook her head. 'We've got plenty to eat in the moana, enough for everyone.'

'Shuddup!' Toroa honked. 'Let's get 'em!'

That day, the land birds watched the sky darken. A huge cloud rushed towards them. No, it was a flock of shrieking seabirds!

Toroa, Sea Kawau and their army swooped. Feathers flew, but the land birds were fighting on home turf, and they sent the seabirds packing forever.

Land Kawau made Tītī stay behind in case the seabirds ever attacked again. 'You can go to the moana for a feed, but your chicks stay here with us.'

Tītī sighed. 'What a bunch of bird brains! I always said there's enough kai for everyone.'

Too right, Tītī. On the bright side, I bet all those feathers lying around after the battle made an awesome kahu huruhuru.

Ko te Whakatau Nui a Willie Apiata

Willie Apiata and the Tough Decision

NZSAS uniform

Check this out. It's a uniform worn by people in a special group in the Army called the New Zealand Special Air Services, the NZSAS. This one here tells a tale of courage and bravery. It belongs to a famous soldier, Willie Apiata, a humble man from Ngā Puhi, who was born in Mangakino and raised in Te Whānau-a-Apanui.

And one night, in a place far from home, he had to make a tough decision.

STORY RETOLD BY MATTHEW GRAINGER
ARTWORK BY MUNRO TE WHATA

Not too long ago, Willie was fighting in Afghanistan. He was sleeping on the hood of his vehicle. He was probably hoping the enemy wasn't close. Hoping it was safe to sleep.

But it wasn't. The enemy had snuck up on them, and suddenly ...

BOOM!

Willie was blown off his vehicle by a rocket-propelled grenade.

BOOM! BOOM!

More grenades exploded as Willie and his comrades dived for cover. Machine guns started firing bullets at them.

RAT-TAT-TAT-TAT-TAT!

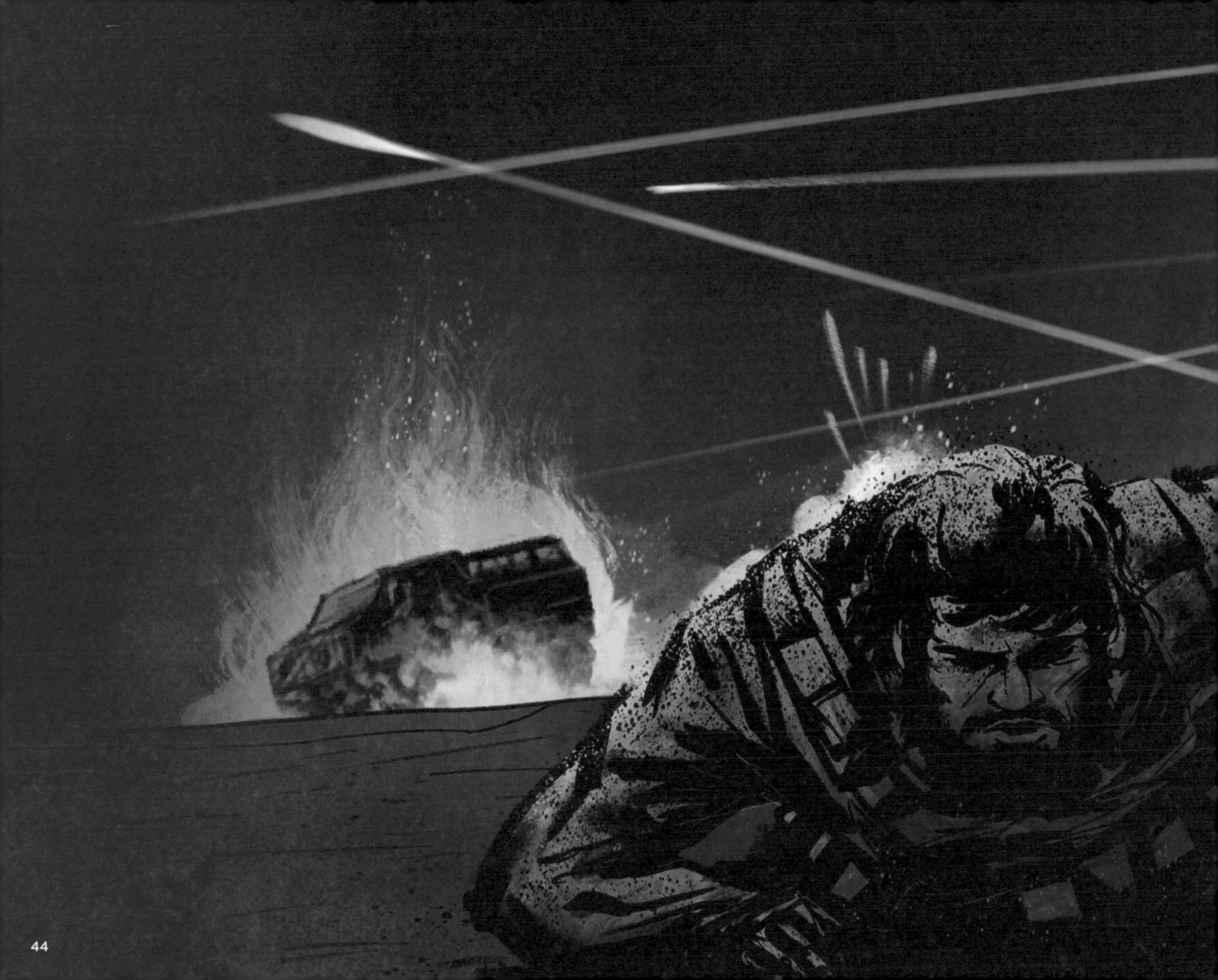

Willie was dazed but wasn't hurt. Then he saw that his Corporal had been hit by some shrapnel from a grenade.

Willie knew that if they stayed where they were, they might get killed. And if he and his Corporal tried to make a run for it ... they might get killed. They were trapped.

But his Corporal was getting worse. If someone didn't do something soon, he was probably going to die.

So Willie made a tough decision. Even if it meant he got killed, it was worth the risk.

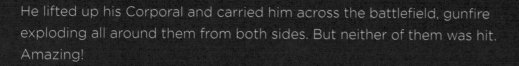

He lifted up his Corporal and carried him across the battlefield, gunfire exploding all around them from both sides. But neither of them was hit. Amazing!

After he made sure his Corporal was safe, Willie returned to the battle and helped drive off the attackers.

For being so courageous, Willie was awarded the Victoria Cross – that's the highest honour someone in the Army in Aotearoa can get. You've got to be the bravest of the brave.

But he was still the humble man from Ngā Puhi:

'I just did what I was trained to do,' Willie would say. 'It's what mates do for each other.'

The sights and the sounds of war never leave a lot of soldiers. And Willie will never forget that night, when all felt lost, and he made the decision to risk everything to save his comrade.

Ko Hēni me te Pakanga ki Pukehinahina

Hēni and the Battle of Gate Pā

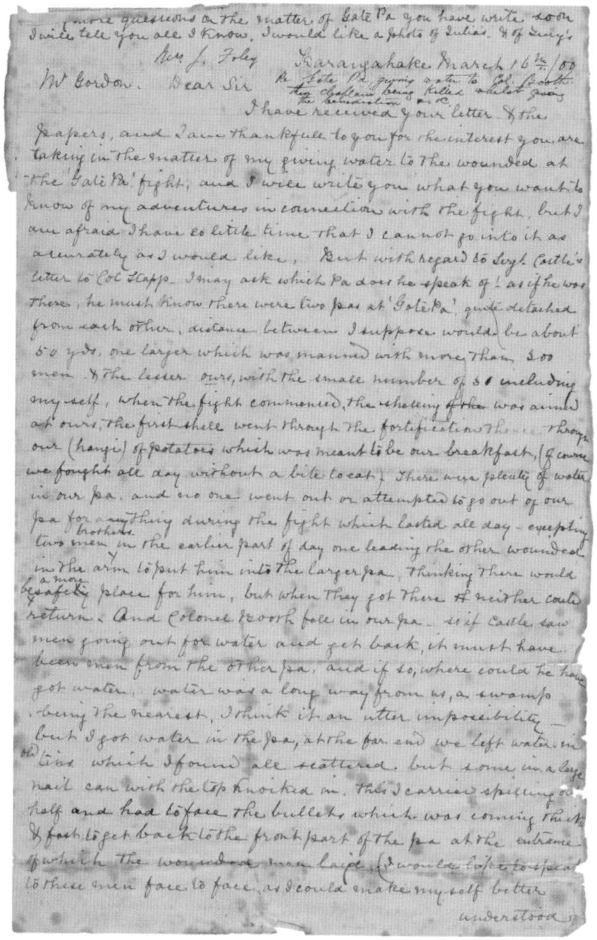
more questions on the matter of Gate Pa you have write soon
I will tell you all I know, I would like a photo of Julia's & of Lucy's
Mrs J. Foley Karangahake March 16th/00
Mr Gordon. Dear Sir Re Gate Pa giving water to Col. Booth the Chaplain being killed whilst giving the consolation &c.
I have received your letter & the
papers, and I am thankfull to you for the interest you are
taking in the matter of my giving water to the wounded at
the 'Gate Pa' fight, and I will write you what you want to
know of my adventures in connection with the fight, but I
am afraid I have so little time that I cannot go into it as
accurately as I would like, But with regard to Sergt. Castle's
letter to Col Stapp I may ask which Pa does he speak of! as if he was
there, he must know there were two pas at 'Gate Pa' quite detached
from each other, distance between I suppose would be about
50 yds. one larger which was manned with more than 300
men & the lesser ours, with the small number of 30 including
my self, when the fight commenced, the shelling of the was aimed
at ours, the first shell went through the fortification then through
our (hangi) of potatoes which was meant to be our breakfast, (of course
we fought all day without a bite to eat) There were plenty of water
in our pa. and no one went out or attempted to go out of our
pa for anything during the fight which lasted all day - excepting
two men brothers in the earlier part of day one leading the other wounded
in the arm to put him into the larger pa, thinking there would
be a more safety place for him, but when they got there & neither could
return. And Colonel Booth fell in our pa. so if Castle saw
men going out for water and get back, it must have
been men from the other pa, and if so, where could he have
got water, water was a long way from us, a swamp
being the nearest, I think it an utter impossibility -
but I got water in the pa, at the far end we left water in
the tins which I found all scattered. but some in a large
nail can with the top knocked in. this I carried spilling out
half and had to face the bullets which was coming thick
& fast to get back to the front part of the pa at the entrance
of which the wounded men laid. (I would like to speak
to these men face to face, as I could make my self better
understood)

Hēni's letter

This isn't just any letter – this letter was written by a woman who was at one of New Zealand's most famous battles. She sent it to an artist who made records of historical events, so her story could be told.

STORY RETOLD BY MATTHEW GRAINGER WITH THE KIND SUPPORT OF TE ARAWA, NGĀTI UENUKU-KŌPAKO AND NGĀTI HINEPARE

ARTWORK BY TE HANA GOODYER

Hēni te Kiri Karamu of Ngāti Uenuku Kōpako was a descendant of the great tohunga Ngātoroirangi himself. Her mum was the daughter of a Māori chief and her dad was from Ireland, the captain of a whaling ship. By 1864, Hēni had already had lots of adventures.

Then she became a supporter of Kīngitanga. They thought that if there was a Māori King, just like there was a Queen of England, Māori would be treated better by the British. The British didn't like this and tried to stop Kīngitanga by attacking the Māori King.

There were major battles and eventually the King, Matutaera Tāwhiao, and his fighters fled into the bush, in what we now call King Country.

Hēni joined them. Her job was to help make their pā strong enough to hold back the British. That was how she found herself at Pukehinahina, or Gate Pā.

The British attacked. There were over fifteen hundred British fighters and just over two hundred Māori. The British leader, Lieutenant Colonel Booth, thought they'd win for sure.

But the Māori King's people, including Hēni, had been very clever when they built Gate Pā, and they managed to defeat the British.

After the battle, as she got ready to leave the pā, Hēni could hear that the wounded men were suffering.

These men have lost the fight, but they fought bravely, she thought. They should be treated with kindness.

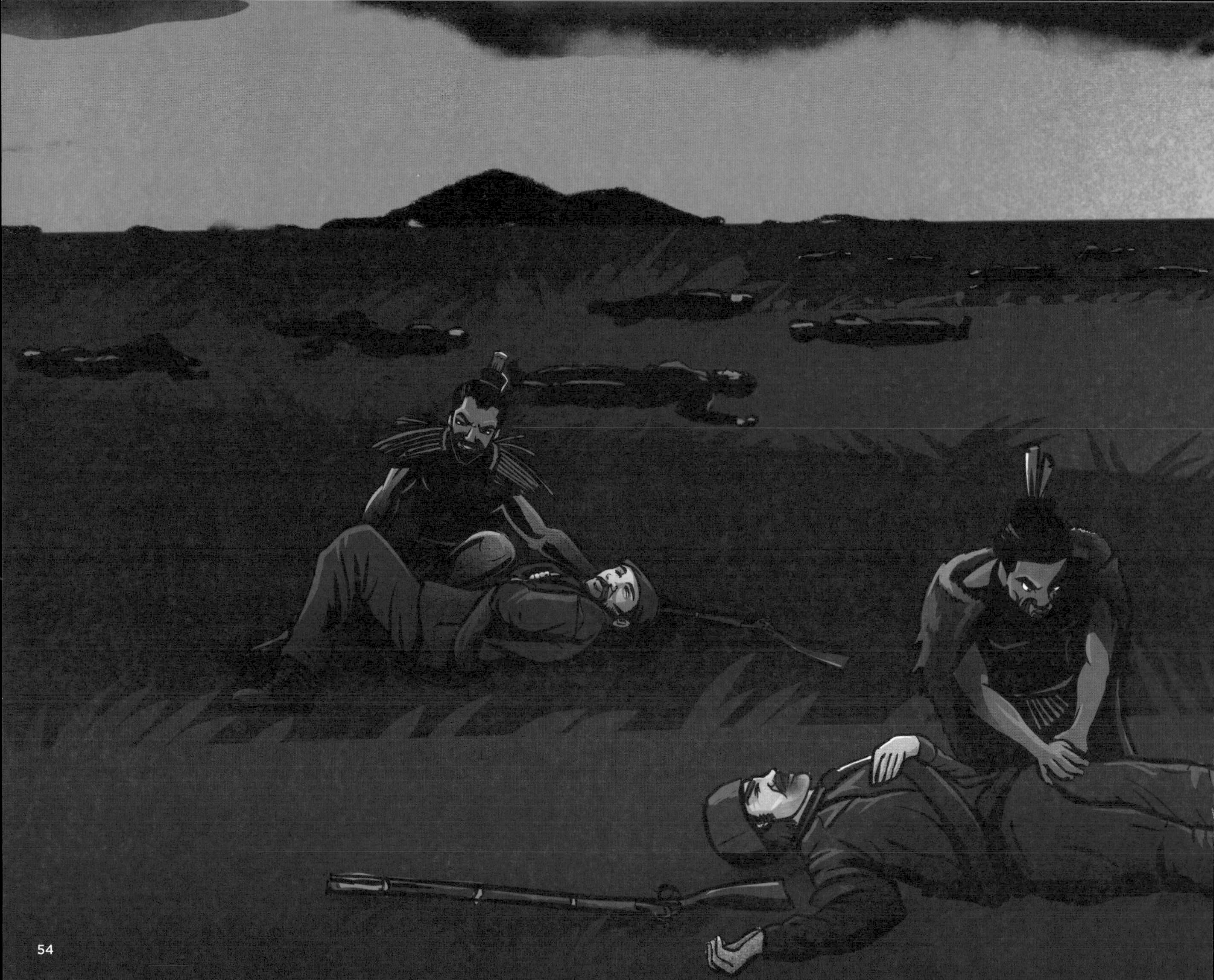

So Hēni brought them water, even giving some to Lieutenant Colonel Booth himself. It was a moment that showed the British forces that Māori were tough fighters but compassionate, too. Word of Hēni's kindness spread far and wide.

This letter was how Hēni told her story, to a man she knew would make sure it was remembered. In the days before email and texts, letters were important – there are some events we only know about now because letters like this survived.

That's why it's a taonga. It means Hēni – and her kindness towards her enemy – will always be remembered.

Ko Rata me ngā Tamariki a Tāne

Rata and the Children of Tāne

Waka tauihu

Can you guess where this carving comes from? A huge waka. Not as big as my waka – that turned into the whole South Island! But isn't it beautiful? It's made of tōtara, the best carving wood. That's what Rata was looking for one day ...

STORY RETOLD BY VICTORIA CLEAL
ARTWORK BY JOSH MORGAN

Rata searched the ngahere until he found the tallest tōtara. 'That'll make an awesome waka,' he thought.

Right away, he swung his toki into the trunk – WHACK. The blade bit over and over until the tree crashed to the ground.

'Nice work.' Rata wiped off his sweat. 'Time to get some kai now.'

He was strolling off when – wait ...

Was that a noise? No – nothing.

Next day, when Rata came back –
'What the heck?!'

The tōtara was upright! He touched
where he'd adzed. Not even the
tiniest cut.

Weird! But Rata didn't think too
hard about it. He really wanted
that waka.

So he hacked and hacked – CRASH. This time, he cut off the branches, too. 'Good luck sticking them back on!' he thought.

Worn out, he started off home.

Listen ... Did he hear something? Nope.

When Rata showed up next morning, the tōtara was upright again.

'Time to get to the bottom of this mystery,' he thought. He cut the tree down again. But this time, when he finished, he hid behind a rock and watched.

Twilight came. Then Rata heard thousands of tiny voices chattering, buzzing. It was the bugs, birds and spirits of the ngahere. Together, they lifted the fallen tōtara, chanting:

Fly together, chips and shavings,
Rise up, noble tōtara,
Child of Tāne, heal!

The rākau was whole again.

Rata jumped up. 'Hey, leave my tree alone!'

'*Your* tree?' squeaked a pekapeka.

'What a nerve!' whined a waeroa. Rata swatted at it.

'It's Tāne Mahuta's tree,' hooted a ruru. 'Rata, have you forgotten?'

A chill crept over Rata. His anger drained away. Auē, he'd been so greedy, he'd forgotten to ask permission from the forest god. Rata plucked a fern frond, kneeled, and laid it before the tōtara.

'Forgive me, Tāne,' he murmured.

And Tāne did. The tree shuddered and fell – a gift.

So Rata got his waka. And every time he launched it, he thanked the forest god.

Āe, a tall tōtara is precious – like this carving.

Next time you're in the ngahere, how about you make Tāne smile: find a big rākau … and give it a hug.

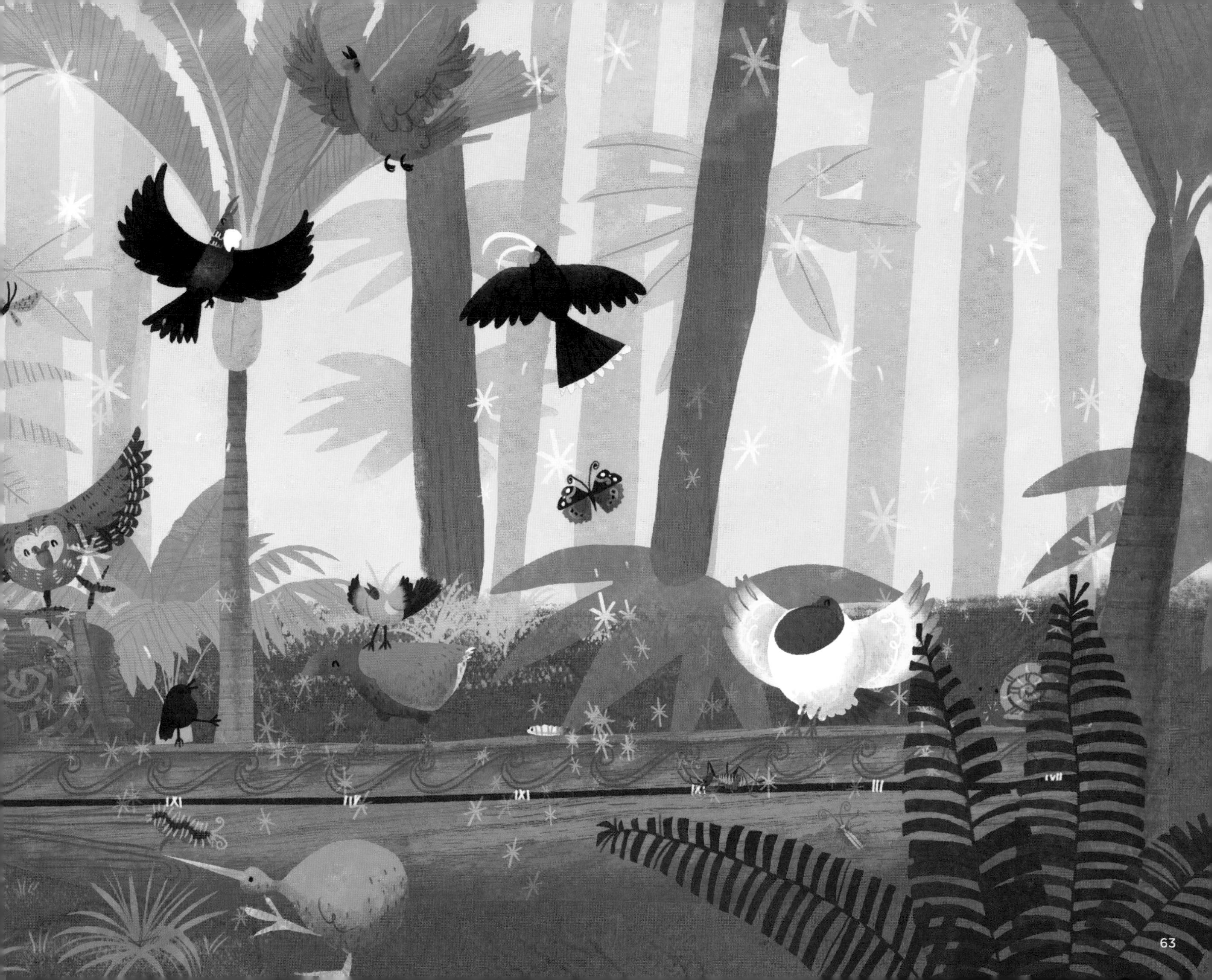

Te Whawhai i te Repo

The Battle in the Swamp

Taiaha

The taiaha is a mighty weapon. This one is made from wood and has three parts: the arero, the upoko, and the tinana.

A taiaha like this one was used by Hapurona, Chief of Te Āti Awa, a warrior who fought another warrior, a Pākehā. They fought each other hand to hand, face to face, eye to eye – and their struggle ended in a surprising way.

STORY RETOLD BY MATTHEW GRAINGER WITH THE KIND SUPPORT OF TE ĀTI AWA
ARTWORK BY MUNRO TE WHATA

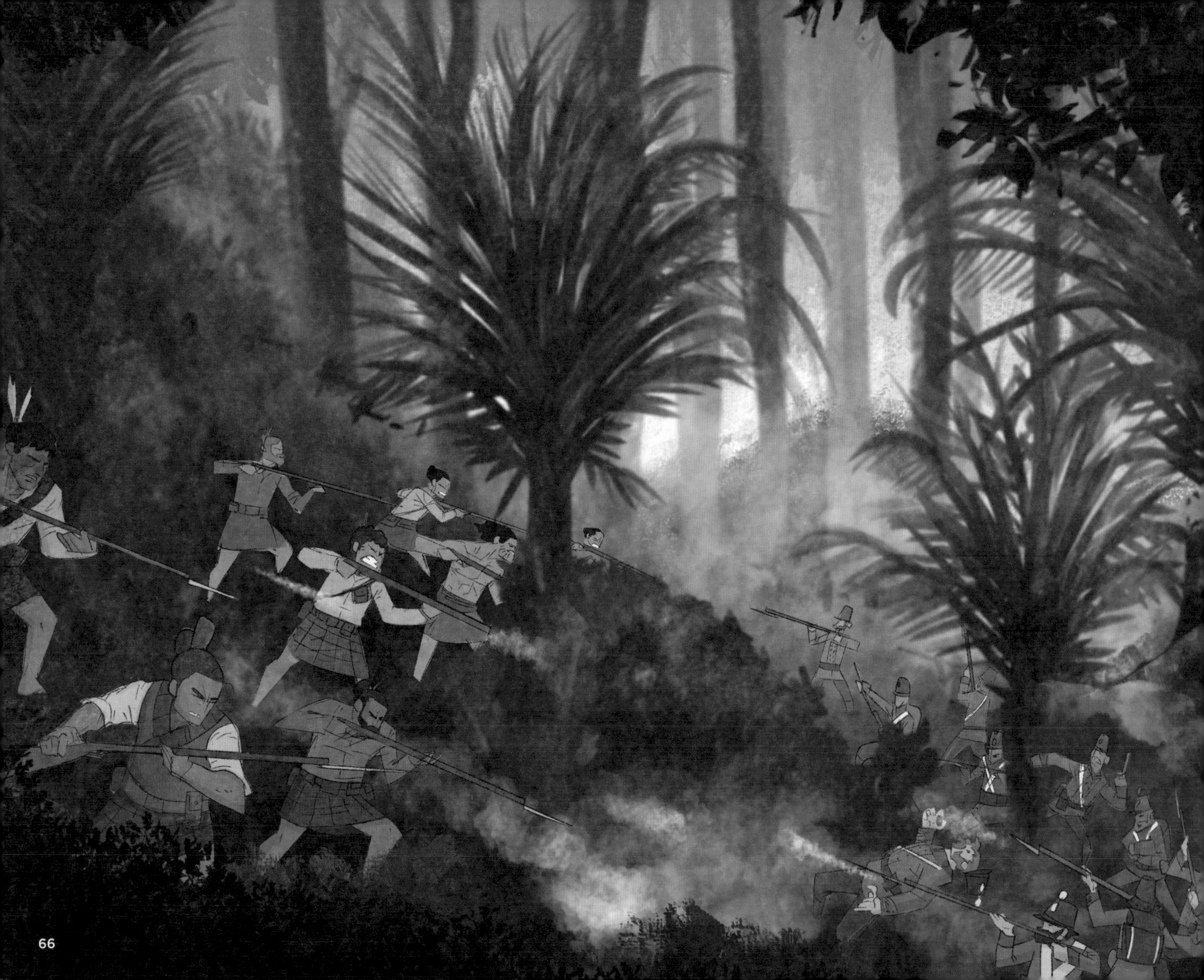

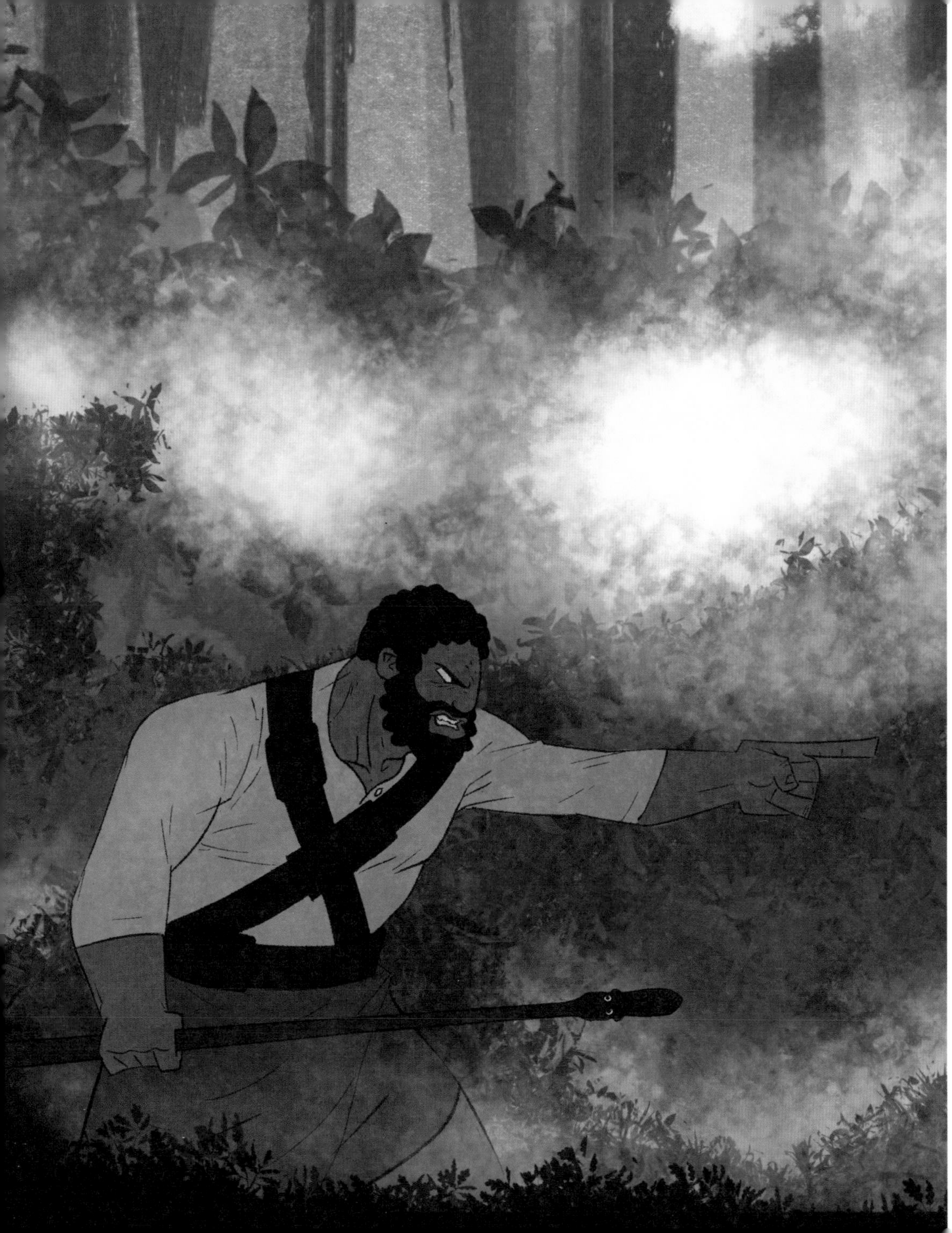

It was 1860. A battle was raging between Māori and British soldiers.

The British soldiers had attacked two pā, Puketakauere and Ōnukukaitara, not far from Waitara.

Hapurona was leading the Māori soldiers, who were fighting back.

The British soldiers thought it would be easy to shoot Hapurona's men. 'We'll teach these Māori a lesson today – they won't know what's hit them.'

But Hapurona was not only a famous warrior, he was also a brilliant war general. And on this day, he outsmarted the Pākehā officers. Many British soldiers were killed. Hapurona and his men began to chase the ones who were left.

Hapurona saw one of them, an officer, trying to run away through a raupō swamp. Hapurona went after him and came face to face with Lieutenant Brook.

Hapurona wielded his taiaha. He had had many years of training. Brook drew his sword, and a great battle began.

But the steel of Brook's sword couldn't defeat the hard wood of Hapurona's taiaha. Hapurona was too strong. His skill with the taiaha was too great.

He struck the Pākehā soldier with his mighty taiaha and Brook fell back into the swamp. He was dead.

Hapurona stood over the body of the soldier he had fought and was overcome with sorrow.

'He fought like a toa, this man,' Hapurona said of his fallen foe. 'I will honour him, my hoariri. I will tangi over the Pākehā I've slain. Haere ki te pō, e hoa!'

And there, in the swamp, Hapurona cried for the brave British soldier he had slain – who had fought so bravely and earned Hapurona's respect.

Māori warriors with taiaha like this one could defeat trained swordsmen with blades of steel. A powerful weapon, in the right hands – and a beautiful taonga.

Kua Mau i te Hau Tonga

Seized by the Cold South Wind

Volcanic rock

See this rock? It's kind of special. It's a volcanic rock, found near Tongariro, a mighty volcano. Tongariro first blew its top after the great tohunga Ngātoroirangi ran into some trouble with Tāwhirimātea, the god of winds.

STORY RETOLD BY MATTHEW GRAINGER WITH THE KIND SUPPORT OF NGĀTI TŪWHARETOA
ARTWORK BY REWETI ARAPERE

Ngātoroirangi left Hawaiki on a great waka and travelled across Te Moana-nui-a-Kiwa. His journey was long and dangerous, but Ngātoroirangi and his people finally arrived in Aotearoa.

They journeyed to the middle of the North Island and saw a spectacular sight. A great maunga to the south.

Ngātoroirangi said, 'I reckon I'll climb this mountain and, when I get to the top, I'll claim it and all the land around it for my people. It'll be our home!'

But it wasn't going to be that easy. Hape-ki-tūārangi had already claimed the mountain.

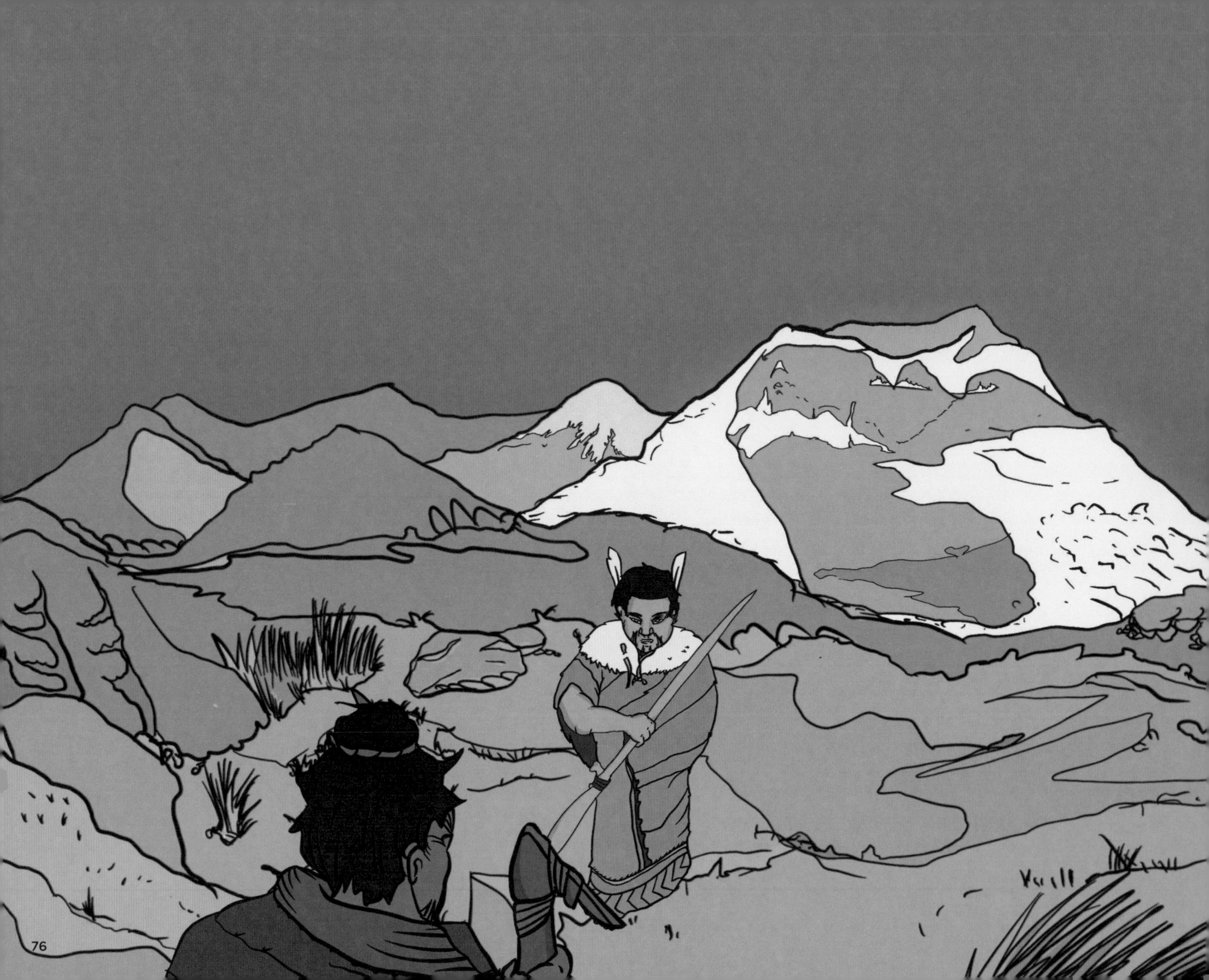

But Hape-ki-tūārangi had never met a tohunga as powerful as Ngātoroirangi, who began to chant – summoning Tāwhirimātea, the god of winds, who sent snow and sleet and icy winds. Hape-ki-tūārangi couldn't survive the cold. Ngātoroirangi had won the mountain.

Or so he thought.

Ngātoroirangi had gone too far. Tāwhirimātea's power was too great for him to bear, and as he and his followers got to the summit, Ngātoroirangi saw that everyone was freezing to death, including him, and he thought, 'Whoa, this isn't good.'

So, with the last of his strength, Ngātoroirangi called out to his sisters back in Hawaiki, 'Kuiwai, Haungaroa, I am seized by the cold south wind. Send me fire!'

Kuiwai and Haungaroa heard him and sent two taniwha to bring Ngātoroirangi the embers of their sacred fire.

The taniwha plunged into the earth and raced to Aotearoa. They found Ngātoroirangi and burst through the mountain top. Ngātoroirangi was saved!

He named the maunga Tongariro.

In time, his people would settle there as Ngāti Tūwharetoa, just as Ngātoroirangi wanted.

Ko Tarakiuta rāua ko Tarakitai

The Tale of Tarakiuta and Tarakitai

Pōtaka

This is a pōtaka, a spinning top that you race across the ground. But this taonga isn't just a toy. It tells a tale of jealousy and revenge, about two chiefs, and a rivalry that led to murder.

STORY RETOLD BY MATTHEW GRAINGER WITH THE KIND SUPPORT OF
TE AITANGA A MĀHAKI TRUST
ARTWORK BY JOSH MORGAN

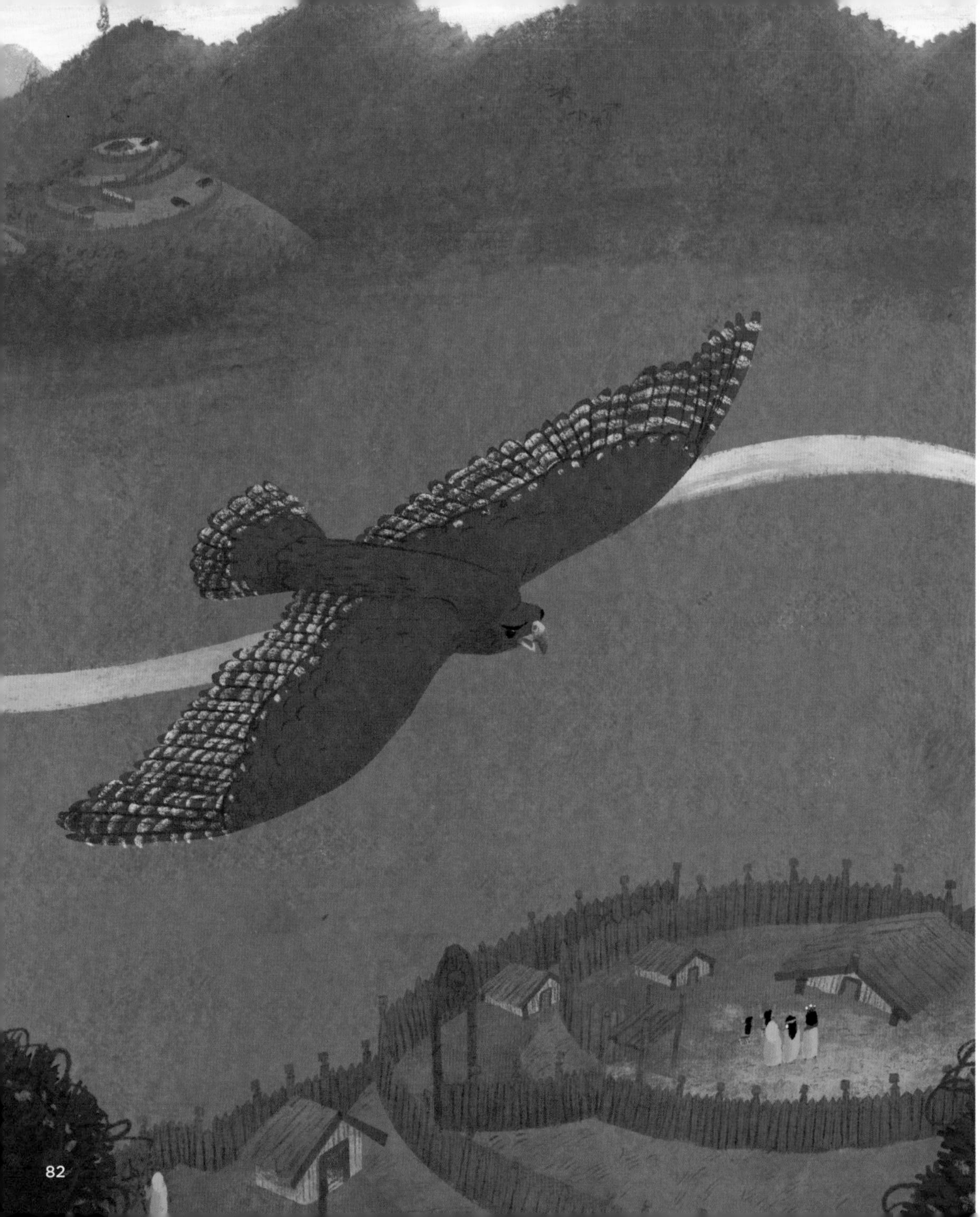

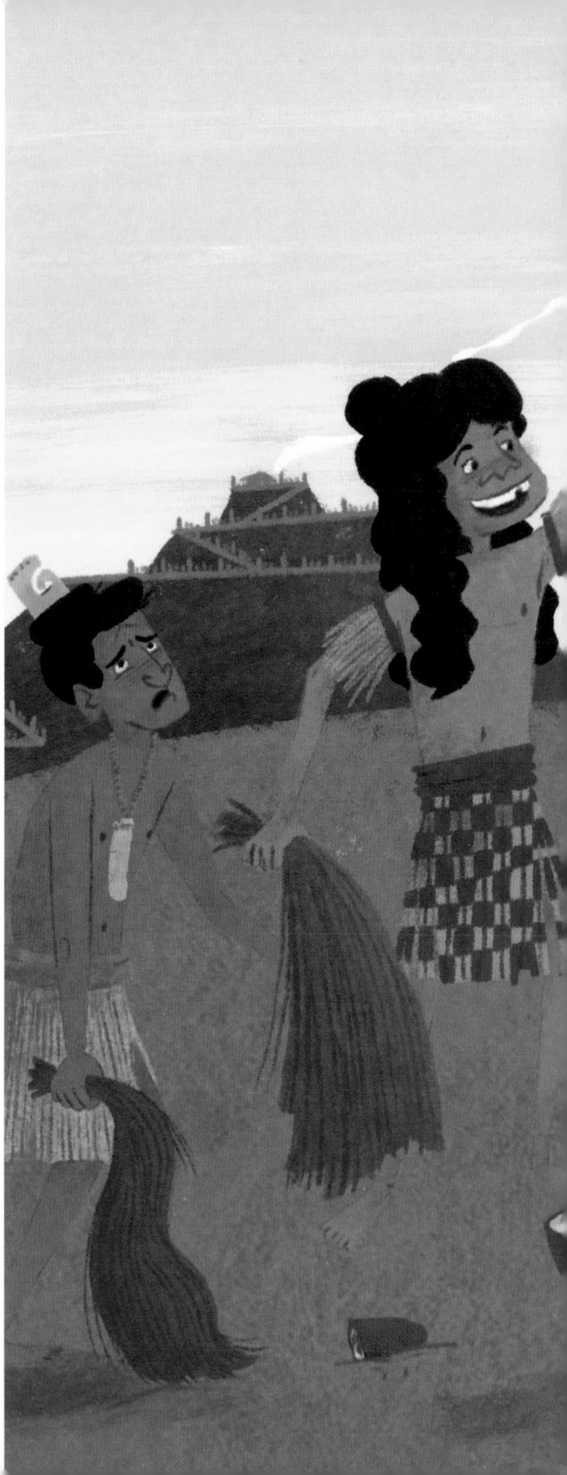

Once, in Tūranga-nui-a-Kiwa, there were two chiefs: Kahutapere and, far across the plains, Rākaihikuroa. The two chiefs were brothers.

Kahutapere had twin sons, Tarakiuta and Tarakitai. Rākaihikuroa had a son, too, Tūpurupuru.

Tarakiuta and Tarakitai were great athletes and the best top spinners around. They were really popular, too, and their people would bring them presents – better than the presents that Tūpurupuru got from his people.

Rākaihikuroa saw that the twins' mana was growing, but his son's mana wasn't. He got jealous. He wanted Tūpurupuru to be chief one day. 'Kotahi te whetū i te rangi, Ko Tūpurupuru,' he said. 'There is only one star in the sky and that is Tūpurupuru.'

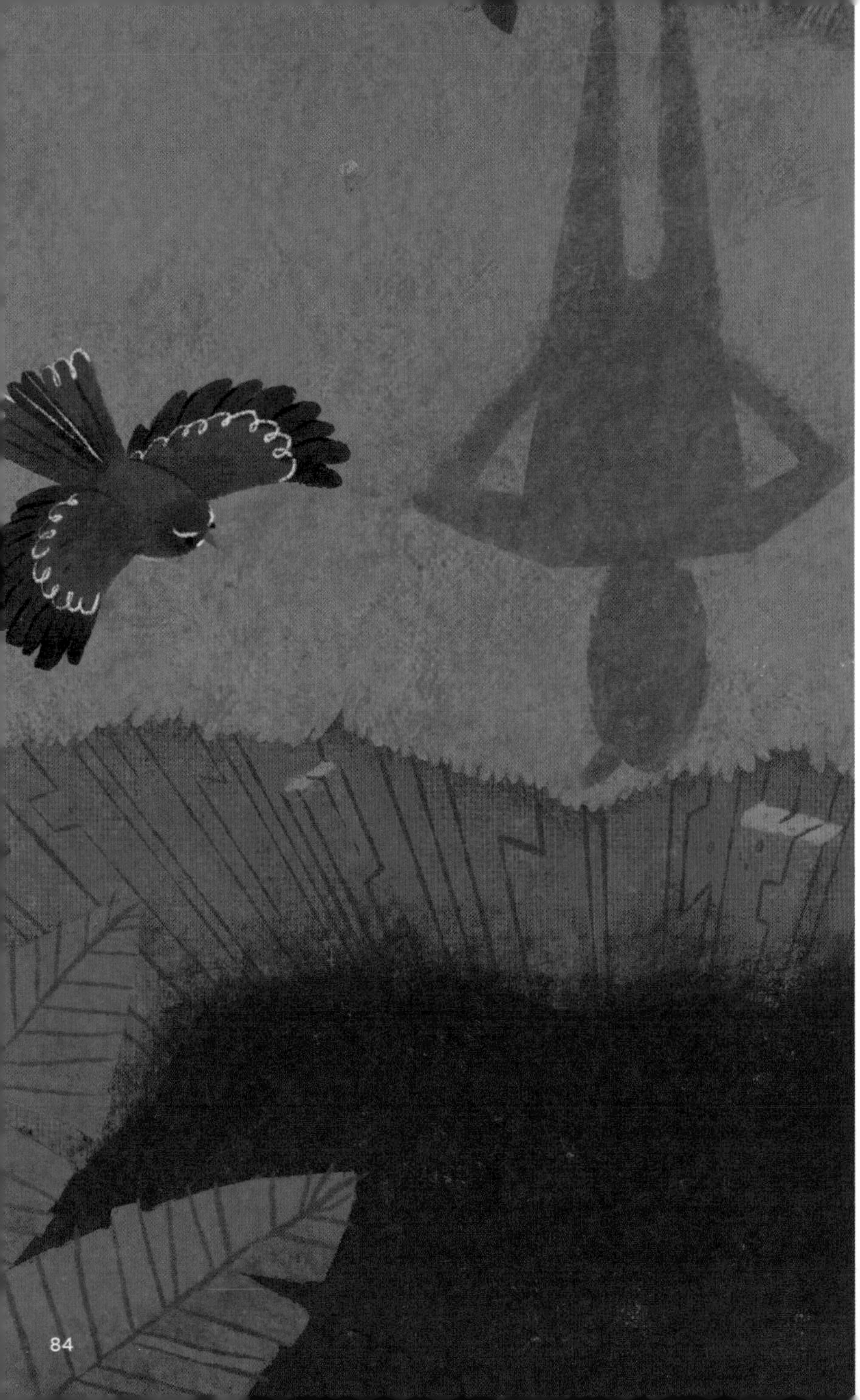

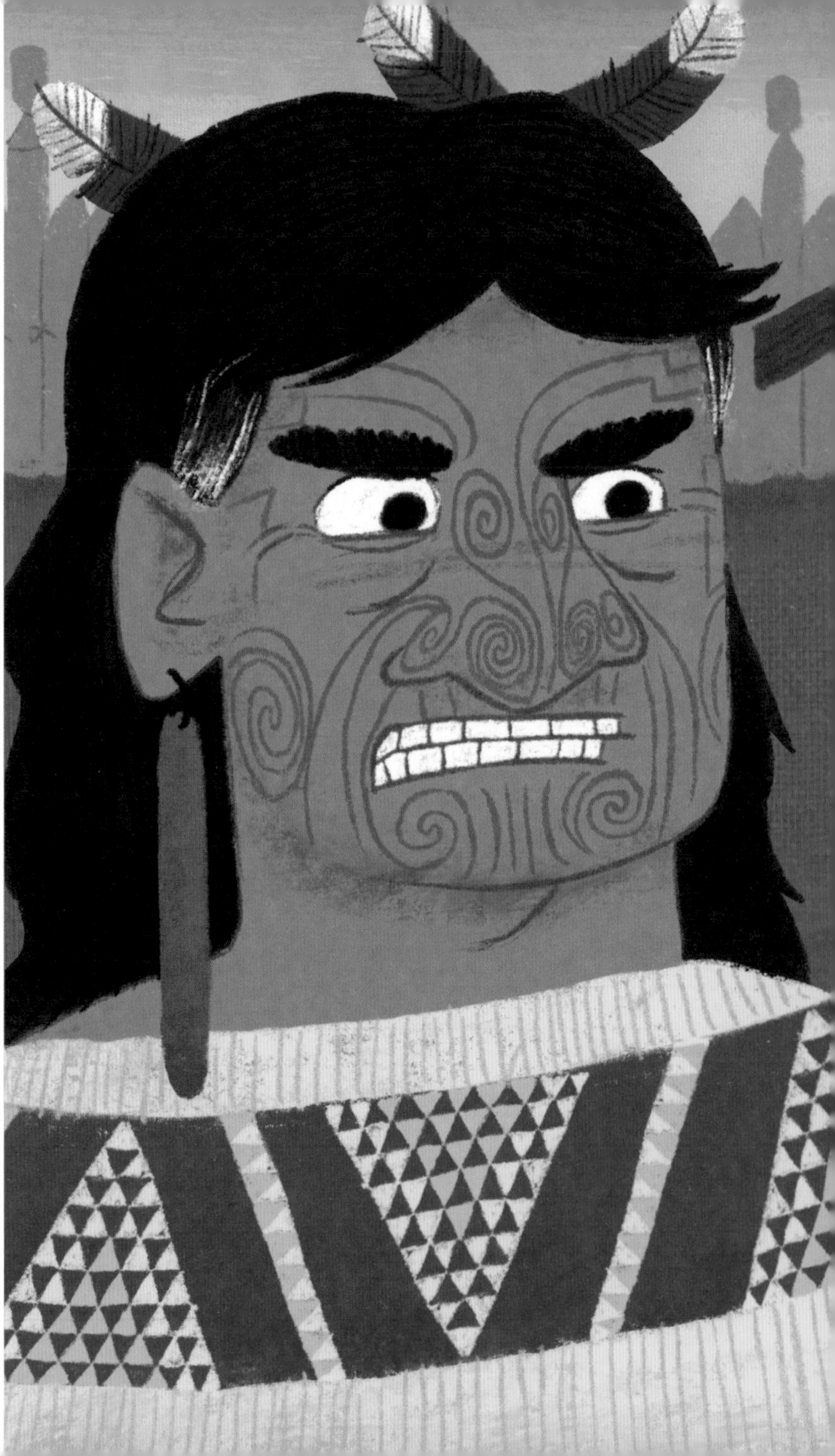

So Rākaihikuroa dug a pit in which to trap his nephews. As the twins spun their pōtaka along a path, Rākaihikuroa lay in wait. He knocked one of the pōtaka into a pit and when the twins jumped in to find it, Rākaihikuroa, their own uncle, killed them.

Kahutapere and his people searched everywhere, but the twins were nowhere to be found.

'My boys wouldn't just run off,' Kahutapere thought. 'Somebody has hurt them.'

And just as Rākaihikuroa had been filled with jealousy, Kahutapere was filled with thoughts of revenge.

'I want to find whoever did this!'

A tohunga made a huge kite and recited karakia, putting his great mana into the kite. He asked the kite to fly to whoever harmed the twins.

The people watched as the kite
soared across the valley, then
dived down ... down ... down,
towards Rākaihikuroa's whare.

Kahutapere and his warriors attacked the pā of Rākaihikuroa. As revenge for the deaths of his sons, Kahutapere killed Tūpurupuru. Rākaihikuroa was forced to flee, his mana in ruins, taking his people with him.

The mana of Kahutapere grew even more. But the jealousy of Rākaihikuroa had cost Kahutapere his beloved sons and brought disaster to both pā. This pōtaka is still here to remind us where jealousy can lead us.

Ko Hinemoa rāua ko Tūtānekai

Hinemoa and Tūtānekai

Kōauau

Whakarongo – this is a kōauau. It sounds like the wind, and it's been known to attract native birds. Āe, it's a powerful taonga puoro. It even lured a chief's daughter on a crazy adventure.

STORY RETOLD BY VICTORIA CLEAL WITH THE KIND SUPPORT OF TE ARAWA AND NGĀ KOROMATUA O NGĀTI WHAKAUE
ARTWORK BY ISOBEL JOY TE AHO-WHITE

A big hui was going on at Rotorua. Everyone was having fun ... everyone except the chief's daughter, Hinemoa. Her dad told her, 'You must sit and be dignified, like the noble puhi you are.' So boring!

Four visiting brothers were showing off for Hinemoa because, actually, she was pretty cute.

She didn't pay much attention – until the youngest, Tūtānekai, began to play his kōauau. That soulful music made her shiver. She was falling in love!

Later, she told Tūtānekai her feelings, and he felt the same way. 'You're the only one for me, Hine,' he said. 'Come to my kāinga and we'll get married.'

'No – he's not good enough for you!' Hinemoa's dad stood between them. 'He'll never be a chief.'

Tūtānekai promised, 'I'll play my kōauau for you every night, Hinemoa!'

Tūtānekai went home to Mokoia Island in Lake Rotorua.

Every night, Hinemoa heard Tūtānekai's kōauau call to her across the water. But she couldn't paddle over – her suspicious dad always pulled up all the waka.

'I'll find another way!' Hinemoa thought. One dark night, she undressed, tied on six hollow gourds, and swam to Mokoia.

'Nice work, Hine,' she thought. Then she looked down. Uh-oh – no clothes! She couldn't show up at Tūtānekai's kāinga like this.

She slipped into a hot pool and wondered what to do.

Footsteps! Someone was coming. Hinemoa's heart thumped. She heard the sound of water being scooped from the pool.

Hinemoa put on a man's voice. 'Give me some wai,' she growled.

'Who's this strange tāne I hear?'

Hinemoa knew that voice. 'Tūtānekai!'

'Hinemoa!'

He wrapped his cloak around her and took her to his whare for the night. In those days, that meant they were married – and even Hine's dad welcomed Tūtānekai.

Later, Hinemoa and Tūtānekai became great tribal leaders. Today, Te Aitanga-a-Tūtānekai is called Ngā Koromatua o Ngāti Whakaue. And on Ōwhata Marae stand the two whare Hinemoa and Tūtānekai, cared for by Ngāti Te Roro o te Rangi. Ka kite anō au i a koe!

Ko te Kaipuke Karihi-Kore

The Rainbow Warrior

Record by Herbs

The song on this record is called 'French Letter' by a reggae band called Herbs, made up of guys from around the Pacific.

They wanted to protect the Pacific and sang a song about it. It was inspired by something that happened right here in Aotearoa, something that made the whole world sit up and go

'Whoa!'

STORY RETOLD BY MATTHEW GRAINGER
ARTWORK BY HURIANA KOPEKE-TE AHO

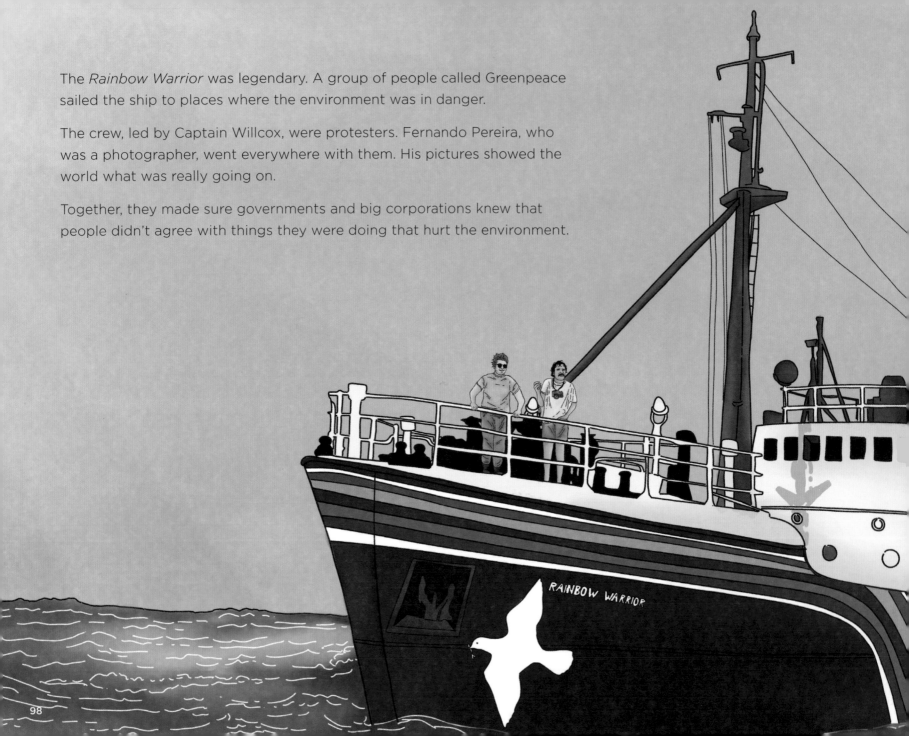

The *Rainbow Warrior* was legendary. A group of people called Greenpeace sailed the ship to places where the environment was in danger.

The crew, led by Captain Willcox, were protesters. Fernando Pereira, who was a photographer, went everywhere with them. His pictures showed the world what was really going on.

Together, they made sure governments and big corporations knew that people didn't agree with things they were doing that hurt the environment.

RAINBOW WARRIOR

Like when the French government started testing nuclear bombs at a Pacific atoll called Moruroa. Nuclear bombs poison the environment and make people sick for years afterwards.

Captain Willcox and his crew knew they needed to try to stop the tests. But the French government got angry. To them, the *Rainbow Warrior* was just causing trouble.

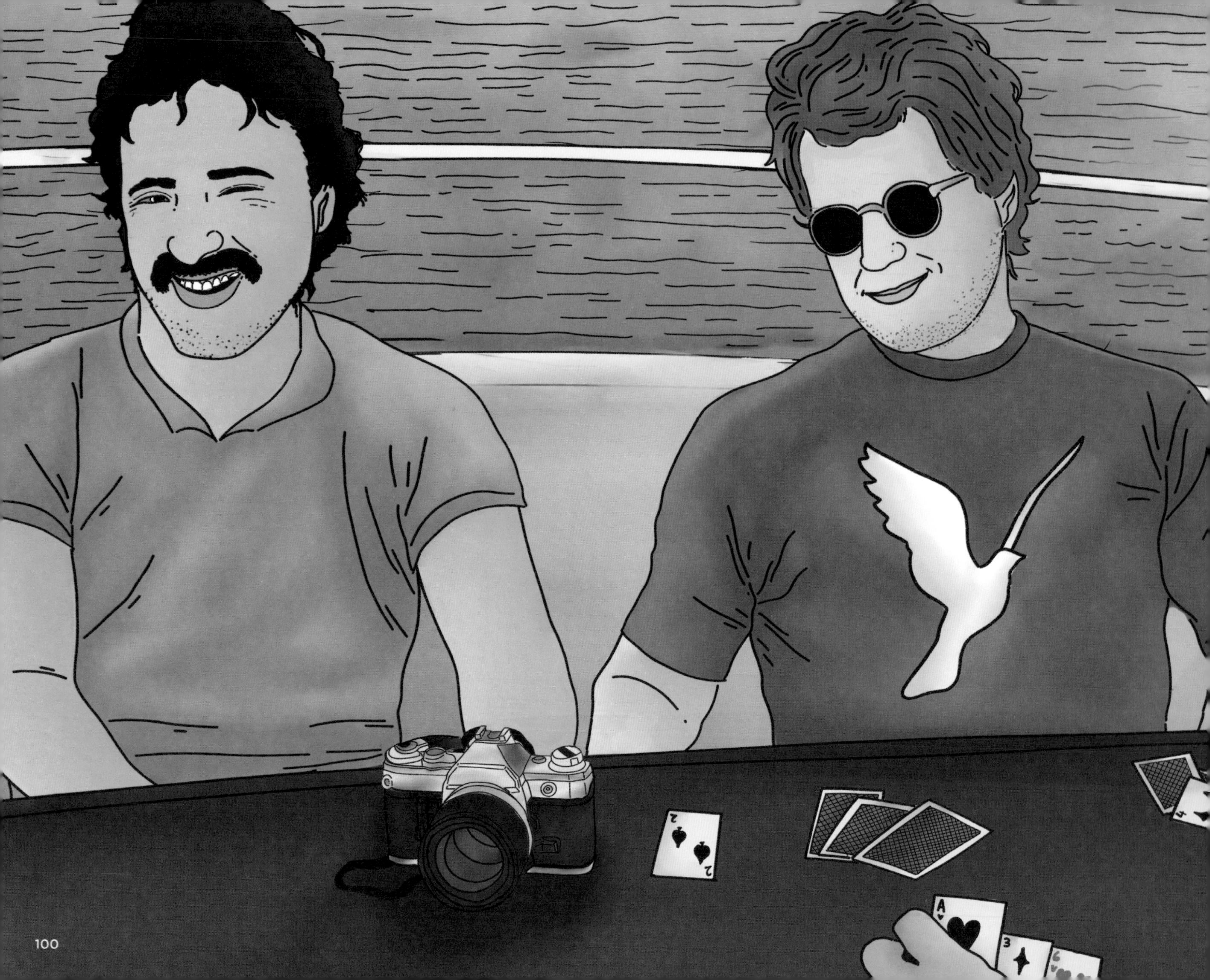

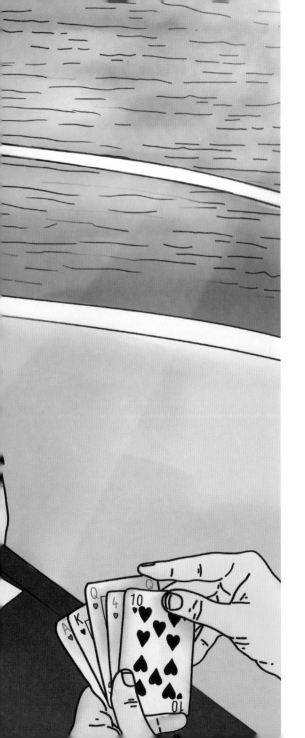

In 1985, the *Warrior* was resting in Waitematā Harbour in Auckland. The crew had spent the day getting ready to head back to Moruroa. A few of them were still awake, playing cards, and celebrating someone's birthday. One of them was Fernando.

The French government wanted to make sure the *Rainbow Warrior* never got in their way again. So their divers put two bombs on the ship's hull.

Suddenly, explosions tore through the ship. Water flooded in. There was panic on board. Everyone scrambled to get off in case the ship sank.

RAINBOW WARRIOR

GREENPEACE

Soon they realised that something terrible had happened. Fernando had drowned because of the explosion. Captain Willcox and the crew were heartbroken.

And the bombing didn't work. Other ships took the *Rainbow Warrior*'s place. Finally, the French stopped testing nuclear bombs right in our backyard, the beautiful Te Moana-nui-a-Kiwa, my home, your home, our home.

Ko Māui me te Ika Nunui

Māui and the Big Catch

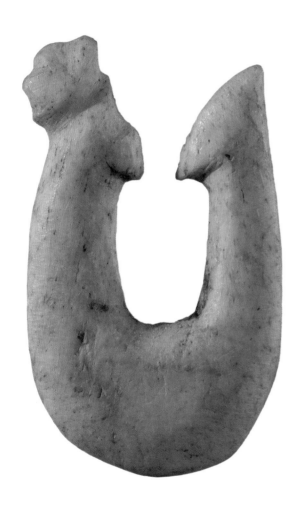

Matau

It takes heaps of concentration to carve a fish hook like this – and real skill to use. And see the bit right at the end? That was my idea: the kāniwha – a barb that made matau better at catching fish.

I've got a pretty special matau myself. I used it to teach my big brothers a lesson they'll never forget.

STORY RETOLD BY MATTHEW GRAINGER
ARTWORK BY MUNRO TE WHATA

My brothers went fishing every day. I really wanted to go, too. 'I'll help you guys!' I'd say. 'Wait till you see all the fish I'm gonna catch!'

And they'd say, 'Only thing you're gonna catch, little brother, is crabs – here on this beach!'

So I came up with a plan to show them they were wrong for not taking me fishing. I was gonna catch a bigger fish than anything they'd ever seen.

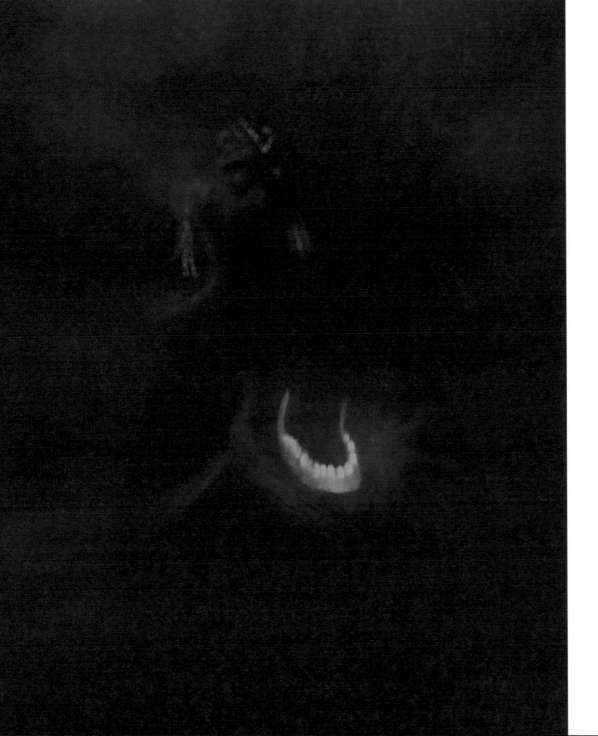

You see, a while back I went to see my kuia, Murirangawhenua, to get her jawbone.

'Kuia! Can I have your jawbone please?' How could she say no to her favourite mokopuna?

That jawbone came in real handy when I used it to slow down the sun. And, watching my brothers head out to sea without me, I had an idea.

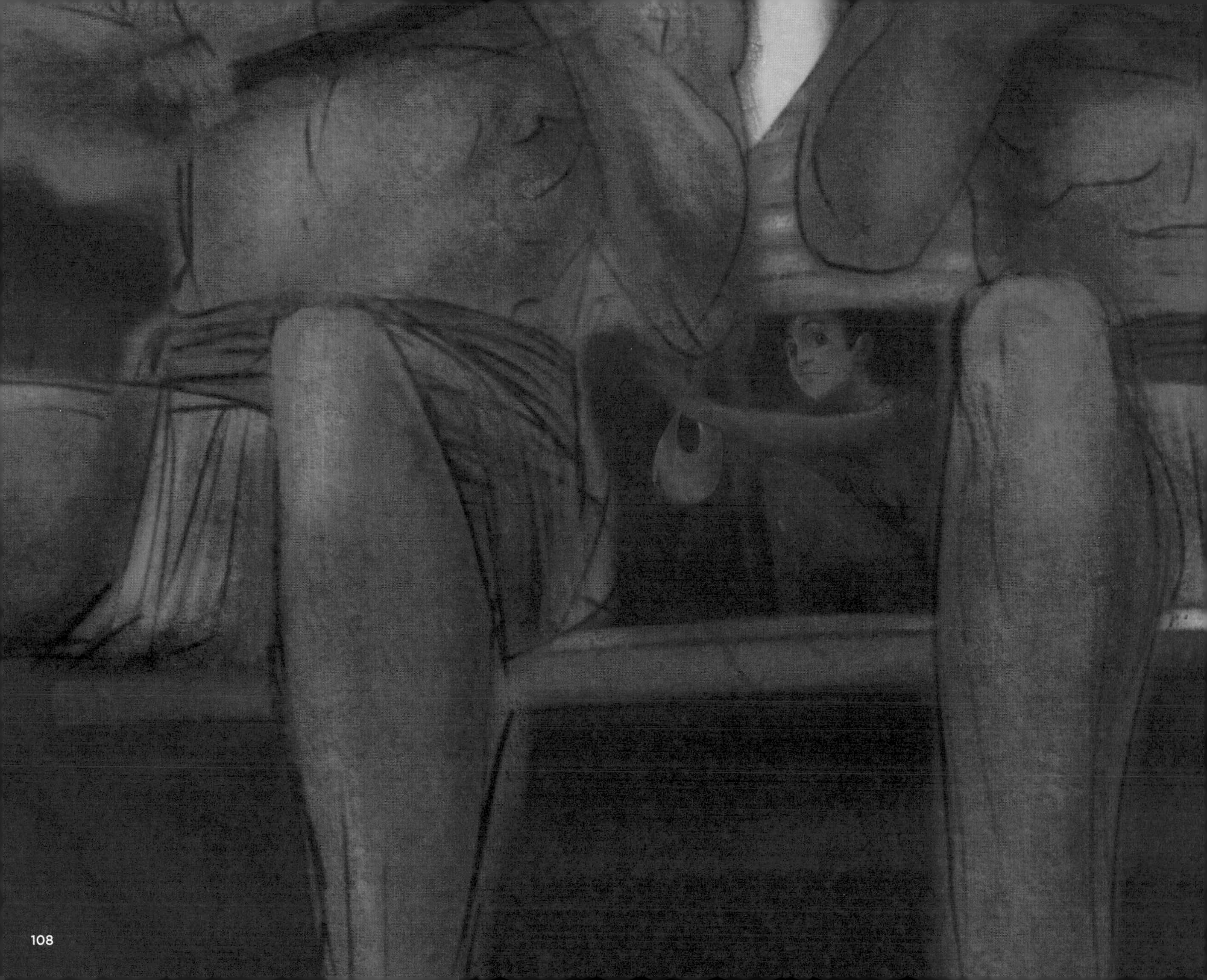

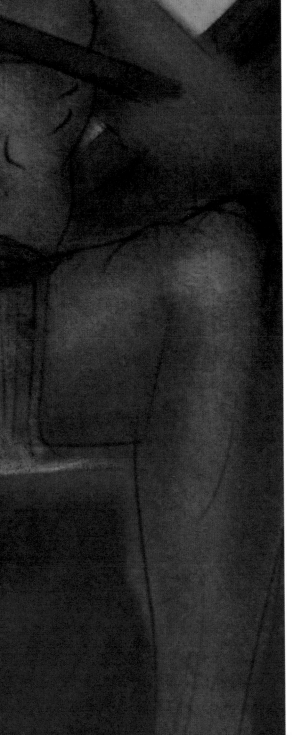

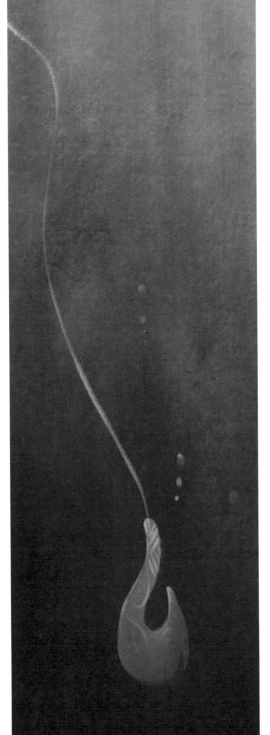

That night I took my kuia's jawbone and made a matau. Not just any matau – a magical one that could catch any fish, no matter how big.

Next day, I hid in my brothers' waka and waited till they were out in the middle of the ocean. Then I popped up and surprised them. They weren't too happy.

'Wanna see fishing?' I said. 'Check this out!' And I threw the magical matau over the side.

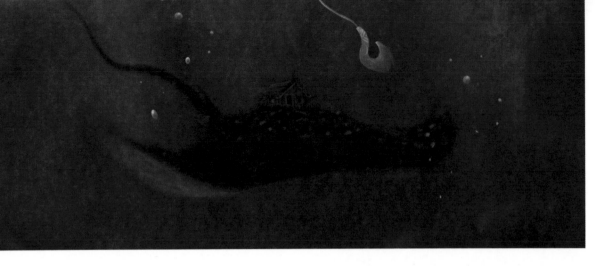

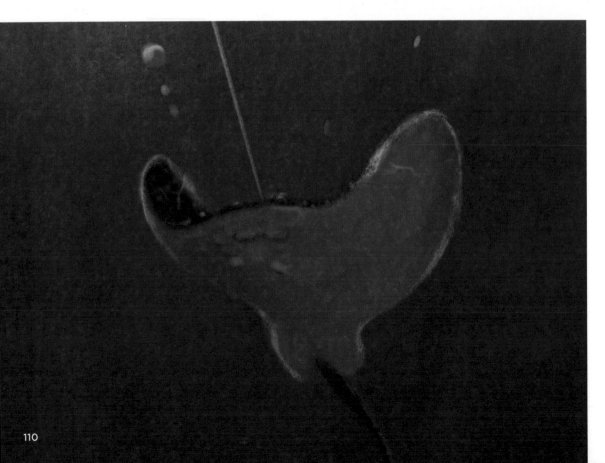

The matau sank down, down, down ... and way down there, it caught on the roof of Tonganui's house. His grandad was Tangaroa, the god of the sea.

I pulled ... and I pulled ... and Tonganui's house came up, along with all the land underneath it.

My brothers caught fish, but my fish was a whole island: Te Ika-a-Māui!

'Whoa!' they all said. 'Nice catch!'

You might know my fish by another name – the North Island of Aotearoa.

Pretty good way to shut your brothers up, eh?

Hey, maybe one day you and I can go fishing. Who knows *what* we'll catch?

Ko Huria me te Kaipuke

Huria and the Shipwreck

Korowai

Imagine being wrapped in this beautiful korowai. You'd feel cosy and safe, right?

It was woven by a chief's granddaughter – Huria Matenga. She lived way back when her people and Pākehā were fighting in the New Zealand Wars. Yet she risked her life to save a Pākehā crew in a shipwreck.

STORY RETOLD BY VICTORIA CLEAL WITH THE KIND SUPPORT OF
TE ĀTI AWA, NGĀTI TAMA, NGĀTI TOA RANGATIRA AND NGĀTI KOATA
ARTWORK BY ARIKI BRIGHTWELL

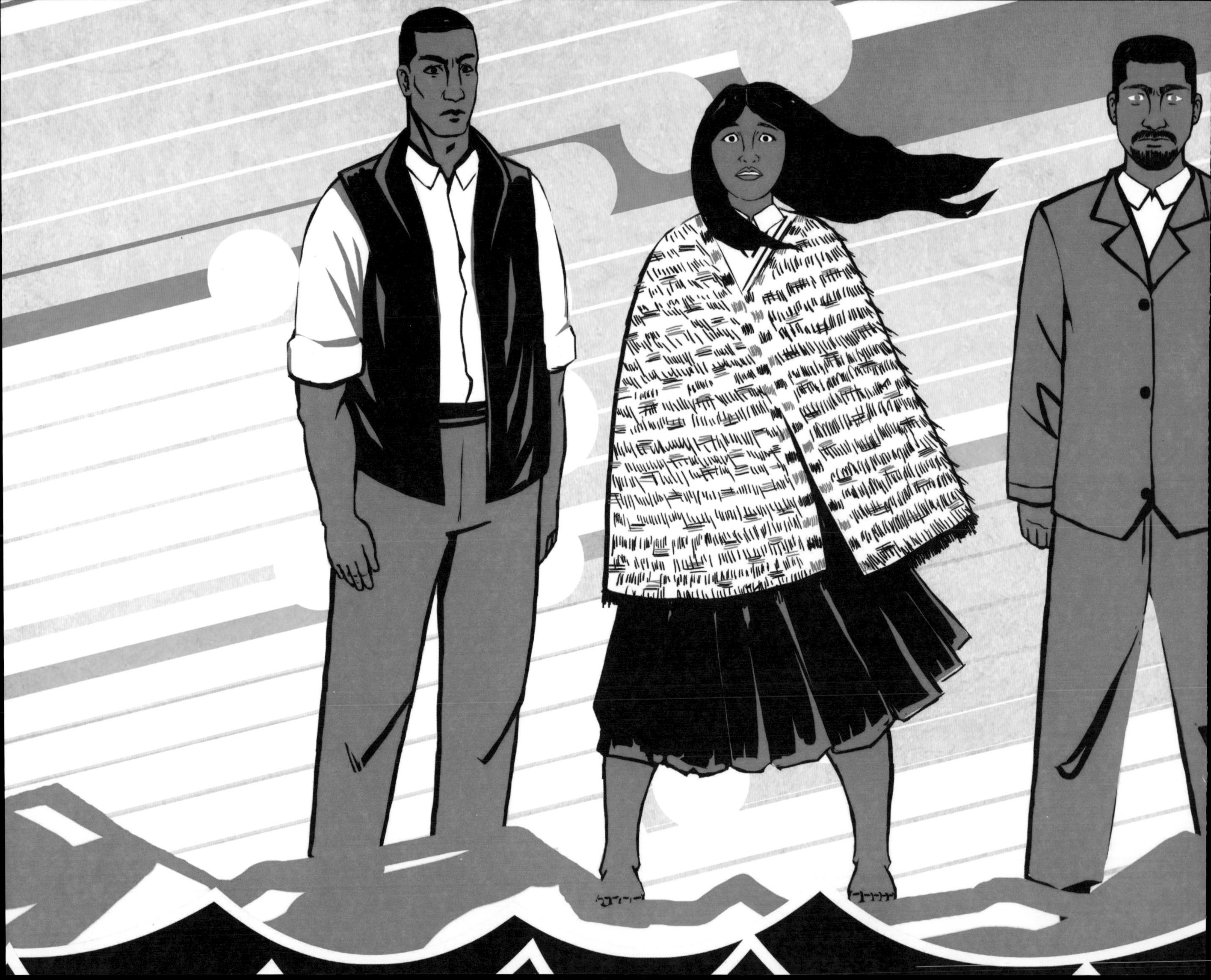

Just after dawn one spring morning near Nelson, a storm raged. On the beach, Huria and her family watched as a sailing ship lurched and crashed into the rocks. Huria gasped. She could see that the sailors on board the *Delaware* were in terrible danger.

Huria's husband, Hemi, pointed. 'Look! One of the crew is swimming to the beach with a rope.' Just as he said this a wave smashed the sailor into the rocks. The other sailors hauled him back on deck.

'They're trapped,' Huria said. 'They need our help!'

Huria threw off her korowai, ran down the beach and then stopped at the surf's edge. She heard the crew's cries for help and plunged into the sea.

Hemi saw his wife take on mighty Tangaroa and knew he had to help, too. 'Come on, Ropata!' he shouted to his cousin.

Angry waves pushed Huria back but she fought on. The captain threw her a rope. Huria, Hemi and Ropata swam with it back to the beach and tied it to a rock.

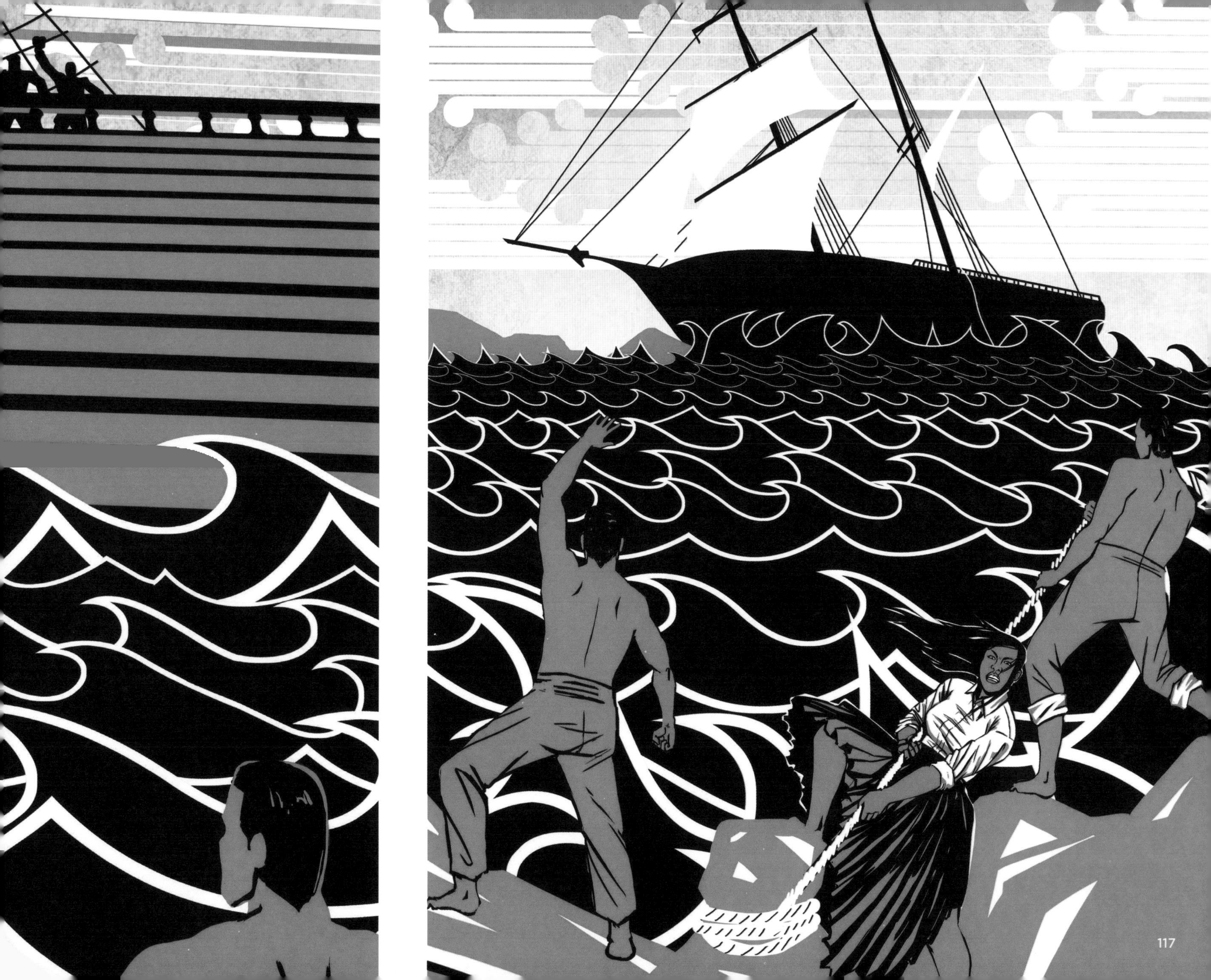

The ship's men hauled themselves along the rope towards shore. Huria, Hemi and Ropata helped them ashore. On land, Huria covered each of them with her korowai.

The captain waited until all his men were off the ship and then made his way along the rope. But it was chafing against the rock. Come on, captain, you can make it!

Then the rope snapped! The captain fell into the waves. Luckily, he was close to shore and could wade in. But was he the last survivor?

Huria looked around. 'Where's the young man you hauled back?'

The captain shook his head. 'Poor Henry was killed. We had to leave him.'

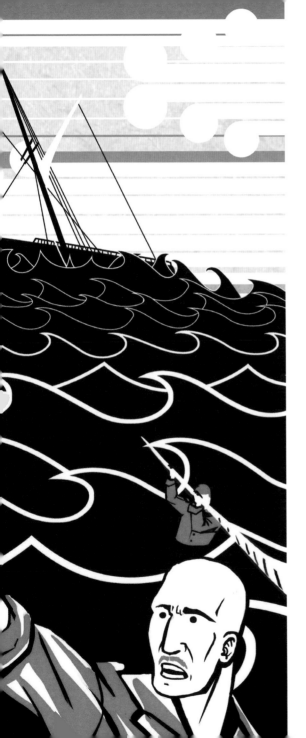

The waves, huge now, clawed at the ship. Huria saw a man appear on deck and wave – Henry!

Then came the biggest wave of all, leaping right over the ship. When it washed away, Henry was gone.

Huria hung her head. She felt the soft weight of her korowai as Hemi draped it over her. 'Without you, Huria, it would be ten souls lost, not one.'

Look closer at the korowai. See how Huria wove harakeke fibre together with wool? Her bravery wove Māori and Pākehā together, too.

Te Paea me te Waka Wairua

Te Paea and the Ghost Waka

Photo of Te Paea's whare

This whare doesn't look that big or strong, does it? It's hard to believe that, once, that raupō roof saved lots of people's lives.

A kuia called Te Paea Hinerangi lived here, in Te Wairoa village, next to a volcano: Tarawera. But one day, everyone got a massive surprise. And not a nice one.

STORY RETOLD BY FRANCES SAMUEL WITH THE KIND SUPPORT OF TE ARAWA AND NGĀTI RUAHINE

ARTWORK BY TE HANA GOODYER

Te Ōtūkapuarangi and Te Tarata, the Pink and White Terraces – ancient volcanic formations. Spectacular, ne?

And in 1886, nobody knew them better than Te Paea Hinerangi, a great woman who descended from Ngā Ruahine Rangi, Ngā Puhi and Tūhourangi Ngāti Wāhiao. Te Paea took tourists in her boat across Lake Rotomahana to marvel at their beauty.

The terraces lay in the shadow of Mount Tarawera. People said this sacred volcano slept and would never, ever awake.

Oh yes, e hoa mā – there's something else you should know: inside the mountain was an atua named Tamaohoi. He was trapped there by Ngātoroirangi, a powerful tohunga.

It was dark inside the mountain, and boring! Over time, Tamaohoi's anger grew and grew. Now his rage started to boil ...

One day, a chief gathered honey from Tarawera's tapu slopes. 'Don't eat it!' Te Paea told everyone. 'That honey is sacred.' But the honey was so tasty, nobody except Te Paea could resist.

When earthquakes started shaking the land and lightning blazed across the sky over Tarawera, Te Paea knew the mountain was becoming angry.

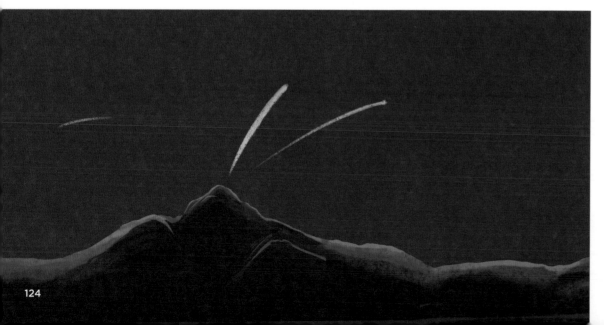

A while later, Te Paea took tourists across Rotomahana. But what's this?! A ghostly waka taua glided through the mists. Whoa!

'This means disaster!' warned the tohunga, Tūhoto. 'It is a waka wairua, a spirit canoe, set free by the earthquakes.'

Soon after, Tarawera awoke! The time had come for Tamaohoi to escape his prison.

Volcanic rocks and ash exploded from the crater. Whole villages were buried.

'Haere mai ki tōku whare!' Te Paea called out from the door of her house.

When the smoke cleared, more than sixty people emerged from her whare – alive! Te Paea and her strong house saved them from Tamaohoi's fury.

Later, Te Paea moved to Whakarewarewa near Rotorua, where she taught other women how to guide tourists, so they, too, could become independent and respected.

But do I hear you asking – will Tarawera ever awake again? E hoa mā, only time will tell.

Te Kauranga Nui a Kahe

Kahe's Epic Swim

Hei tiki

Imagine swimming for hours through the night and through a storm to try to save your family, with your kid strapped to your back and a fleet of enemy waka to dodge. Mīharo!

This hei tiki belonged to a brave wahine toa who did just that.

Think she'll make it?

STORY RETOLD BY JEN CRADDOCK WITH THE KIND SUPPORT OF NGĀTI TOA RANGATIRA
ARTWORK BY MIRIAMA GRACE-SMITH

Kahe was a chief's daughter, and she could swim like a fish. In her home on Kāpiti Island, she beat the guys in races all the time – they just couldn't keep up.

And man, she was built! Six feet tall, super strong, and she could stay underwater for ages at a time. No snorkel or fins back then, eh.

One morning, Patetere came to
her looking as if he'd seen a ghost.
'I had a terrible dream,' he said.
'A war party – heading this way.
Get out of here, or you'll be killed!'

'Really?' thought Kahe. She knew her
father and his friend Te Rauparaha
had enemies, but a dream was just
a dream, right? 'Let's wait and see if
your omen comes true,' she said.

Sure enough, a few nights later, Patetere spotted black dots on the moonlit water, far out to sea. Waka! Heading for the island! He ran to Kahe.

'Escape while you can!' he gasped. 'In the morning it'll be too late!'

Kahe's father and heaps of the village warriors were away on the mainland. She had to warn them. She couldn't paddle a waka or she'd be seen. She would have to swim and take her daughter with her – she couldn't risk Rīpeka falling into the hands of the enemy.

There was no time to lose. The village tohunga covered Kahe with whale oil to help ward off the cold. Then he called on Tangaroa, the god of the sea, and Tāwhirimātea, the god of the winds, to guide her to shore, and tied Rīpeka to her back on a mat of raupō leaves.

133

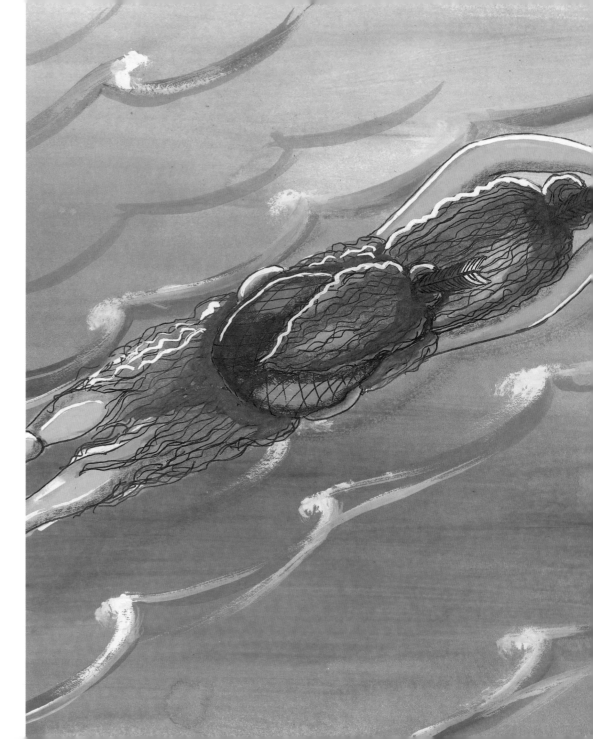

The wind was rising, the current was strong – it could easily drag Kahe off course.

Hour after hour she swam through the darkness. The wind stung her face, and waves pushed her back. Her legs and arms burned. She had to rest. Floating on her belly, she sang to Rīpeka, cold and crying on her back. One last push. 'Come on, Tangaroa, give me a hand!'

Listen! Was it ...? Yes! The sound of breaking waves. Just a little further ...

Kahe was totally exhausted. Who wouldn't be after that? But she and Rīpeka had finally made it, and Kahe could now warn her whānau.

All up, Kahe swam about ten kilometres. She went on to sign the Treaty of Waitangi. True! And today, that stretch of sea is called Te Rau-o-te-Rangi channel, after Kahe's full name. What a wahine toa, ne?

Te Ngarohanga o ngā Parirau o te Kiwi

How the Kiwi Lost Its Wings

Kahu kiwi

What kind of feathers do you think have been used to make this kākahu? Kiwi feathers. Beautiful, but look closer. They're kind of scruffy, eh?
Kiwi can't fly, so he doesn't need smooth huru.

Back in the day, though, Kiwi was an awesome flier.

STORY RETOLD BY VICTORIA CLEAL
ARTWORK BY TE HANA GOODYER

WHOOSH. Kiwi zoomed over the treetops, his wings shining in the sunlight. His buddies were close behind: Tūī, Pūkeko and Pīpīwharauroa.

Those manu were different then, too – Tūī had no white feathers, Pūkeko lived on dry land and Pīpīwharauroa had a nest.

'Haere mai! Haere mai!' The voice of Tāne-hokahoka boomed through the ngahere. He was the guardian of Kiwi and the other manu, so quick-smart they swooped to the forest floor.

Tāne-hokahoka was with his brother Tāne Mahuta, the guardian of the forest, and they looked grim.

Auē! The place was crawling with bugs – scoffing everything, killing the ngahere!

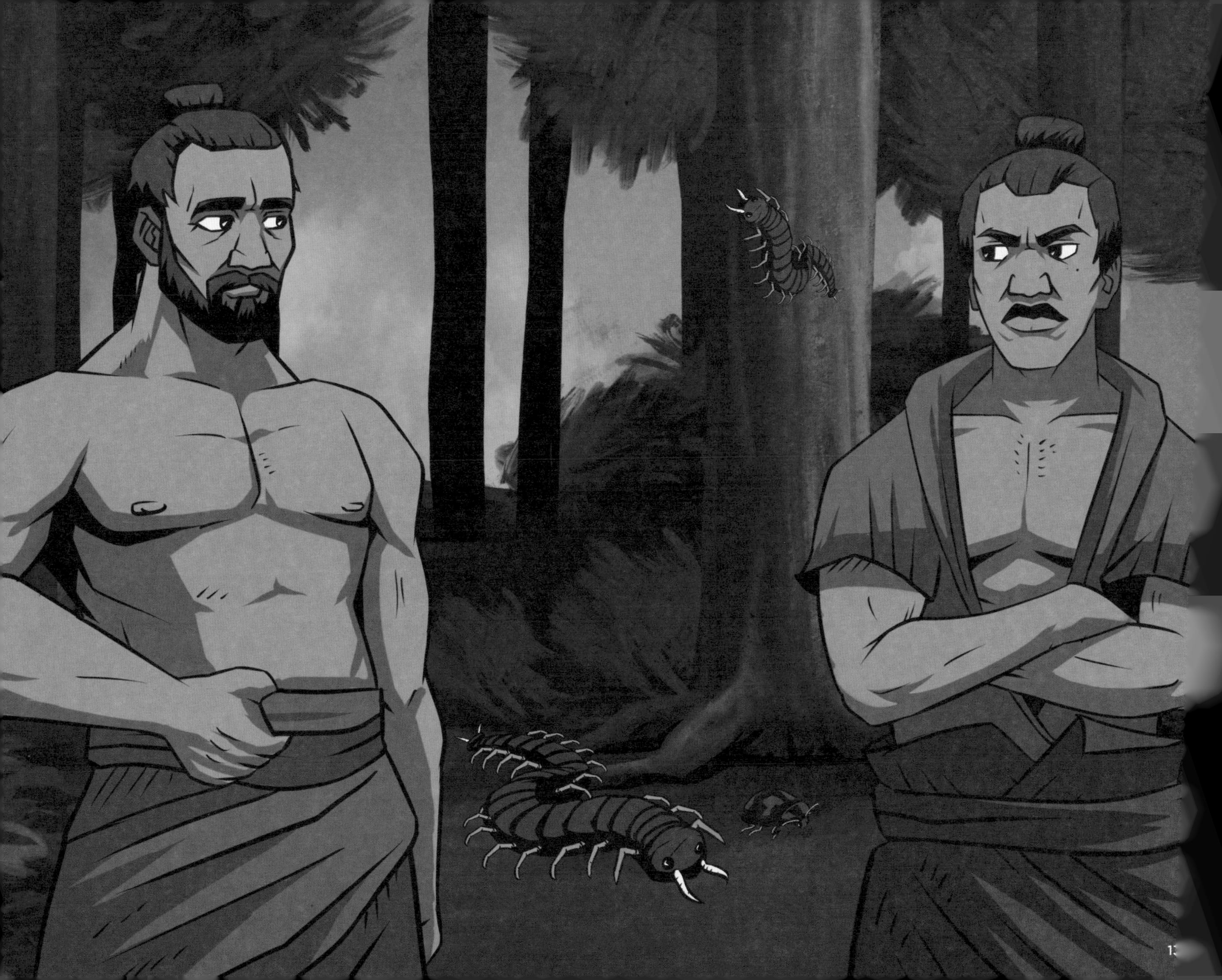

Tāne Mahuta told the manu, 'One of you must eat up these pepeke and bring balance to the forest again. Who'll move down to the ground? Tūī?'

Tūī trembled. 'What if monsters are here? Count me out.'

'Pūkeko,' Tāne Mahuta asked, 'will you help me?'

'Yuck, no!' she said. 'It's too damp – this squelchy mud feels gross between my toes.'

Tāne Mahuta looked at Pīpīwharauroa.

'E hē!' she snapped. 'I'm too busy making a nest.'

Finally, Tāne Mahuta turned to Kiwi. 'Will you, e hoa?'

Kiwi looked at the sunlight above and at his friends. How could he leave everything he loved? And yet, the forest needed him. 'Āe,' he murmured. 'I will.'

Tāne Mahuta knelt before Kiwi. 'You'll no longer be able to fly. Are you sure?'

Kiwi looked at the setting sun and at his friends one last time. 'I'm sure.'

Then his wings began to shrink. His legs thickened and his beak grew.

141

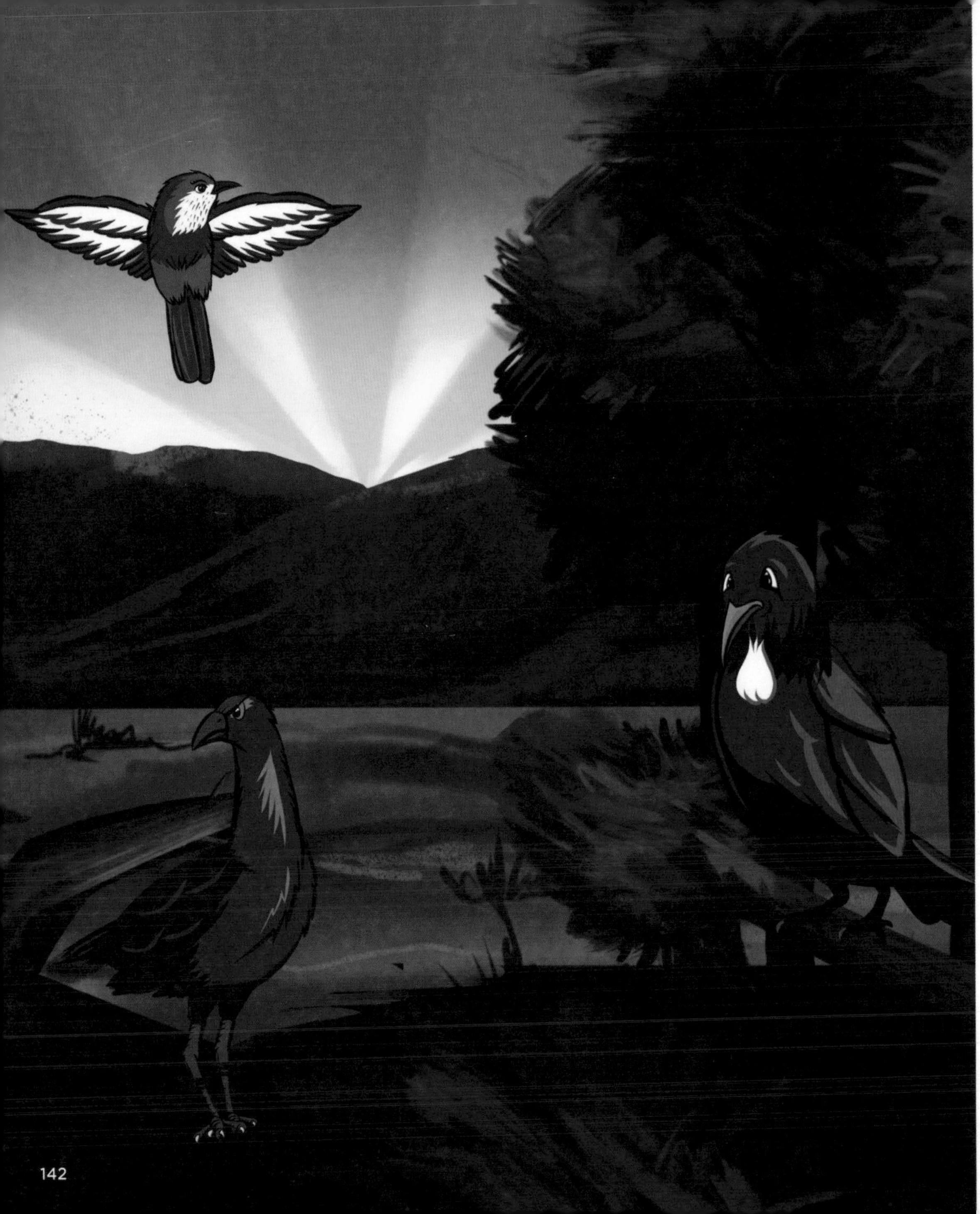

Tāne Mahuta sure was hōhā with those other manu. He gave Tūī white feathers – the mark of a coward. He sent Pūkeko to the squelchy swamp. And he took away the nest of Pīpīwharauroa – now, she lays eggs in the kōhanga of other manu.

And Kiwi? He saved the forest and became Tāne Mahuta's most-loved bird.

He's Aotearoa's favourite manu, too. Hey – when the sun sets, think of our scruffy friend, heading off to keep those bugs in check for another night.

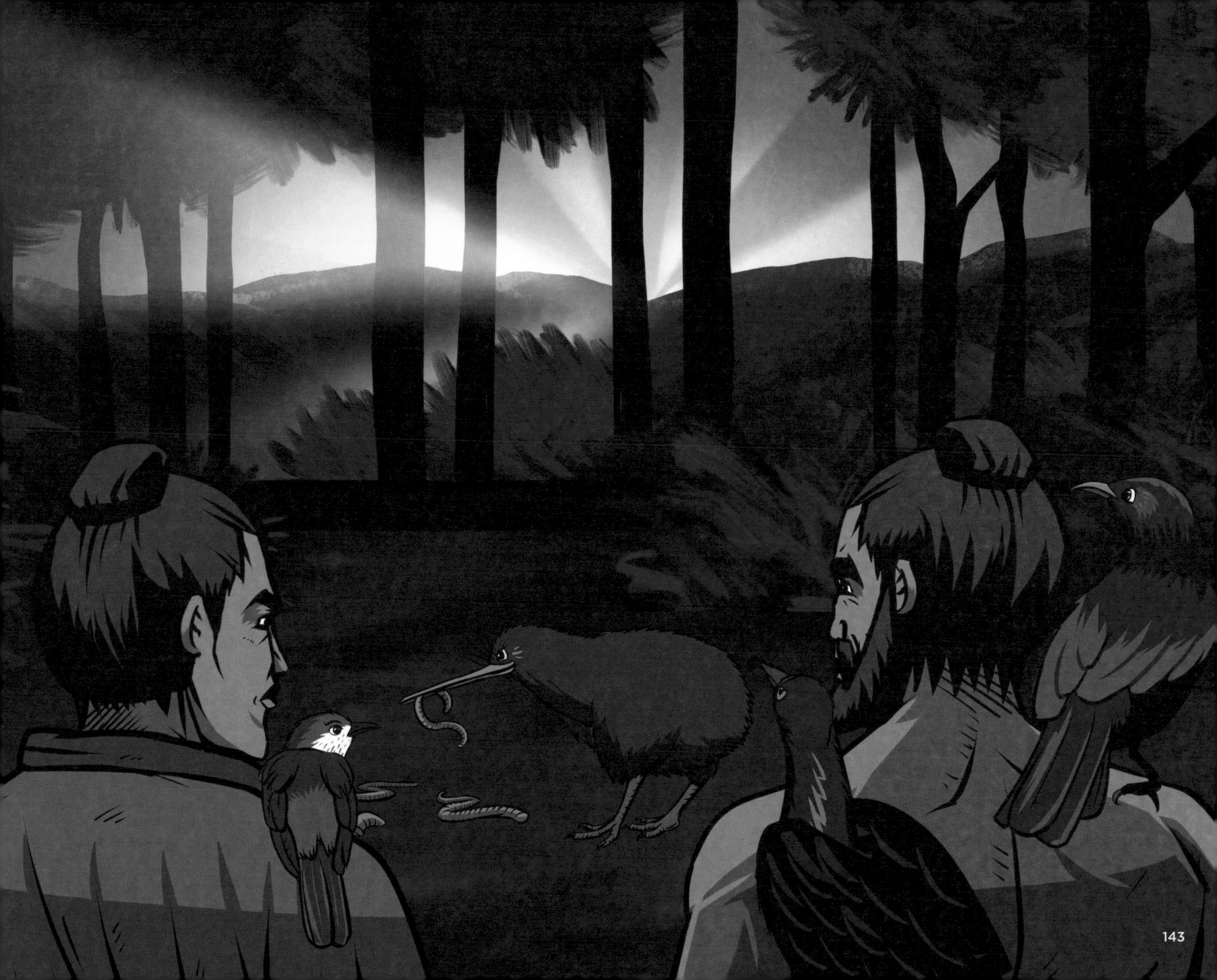

Ko Kupe me te Wheke Nunui

Kupe and the Giant Wheke

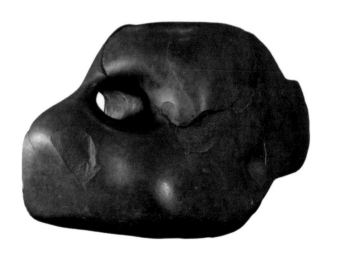

'Maungaroa'

Reckon you could lift this stone? No way! It's heavy for a reason: about a thousand years ago it had to anchor a huge waka in stormy seas.

Its name is Maungaroa and it belonged to Kupe. He was in that waka chasing his sworn enemy across the Pacific. Not a human enemy, though. A slippery dude, with eight arms.

STORY RETOLD BY JEN CRADDOCK
ARTWORK BY MUNRO TE WHATA

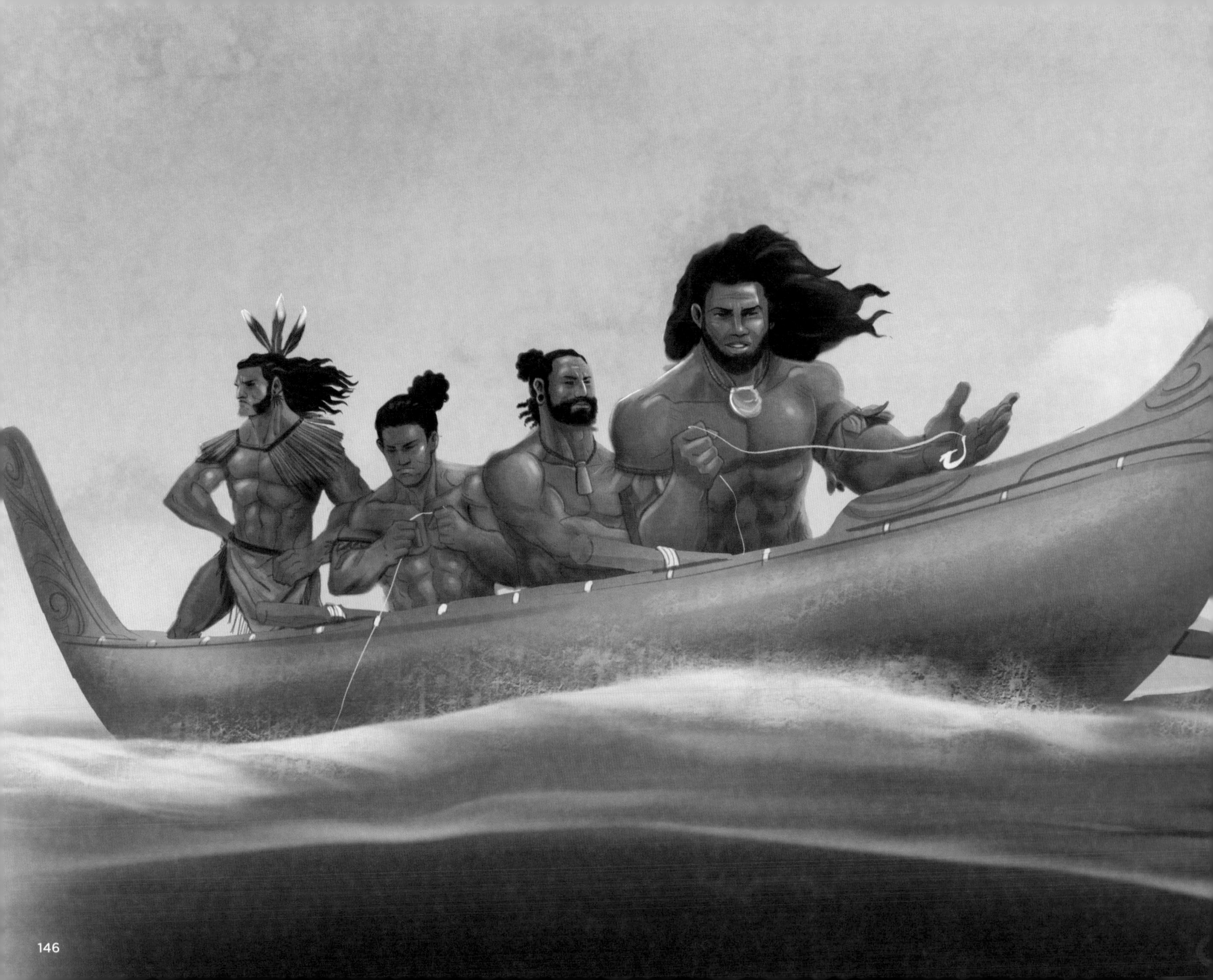

Kupe was a rangatira back in Hawaiki. His people were awesome at fishing. Every day they headed out to sea, and every day their waka came back chocka with fish.

One day, they lowered their lines, and waited ... and waited. Rā, the sun, rose higher. Nothing – not a nibble! One guy pulled up his line. 'Hey, my hook's empty.' The others all did the same. 'Ours too! Who's nicking our bait?'

'I've got a feeling our thief's a slimy sucker,' Kupe said. He'd heard tales of a huge, hungry wheke that a neighbouring tohunga called Muturangi kept as a pet.

When Kupe confronted him, Muturangi laughed. 'You think I tell my wheke what to eat?!'

'Then I'll kill it,' Kupe said. Muturangi grinned. 'Unless it gets you first!'

Kupe's mind was made up. 'Get ready for a long trip,' he told his whānau. They built a waka named *Matahourua* and set sail. The hunt was on!

Out at sea, an enormous tentacle rose dripping from the waves and squeezed the waka tight. Kupe slashed at the tentacle with his mere.

The wheke fled across the waves like a giant sea spider. 'After it!' Kupe yelled.

149

The chase went on for weeks. Then, one morning, Kupe's wife Hine-te-Aparangi gave a shout. 'He aotearoa! A long white cloud!' It wasn't the wheke – it was land! Green, with huge trees. It was awesome, but the wheke was still out there.

Kupe chased the wheke south, and a great battle began. Smash! The wheke's arms lashed the waka like whips. Crack! It tore a hole in the side and water poured in. Kupe thought fast. Water gourds were rolling around his feet. He flung them into the sea.

Mistaking them for bodies, the wheke pounced. Kupe jumped onto its head and thumped his mere down with all his might. 'Take that, Te Wheke o Muturangi!'

Kupe watched the wheke slowly sink. Then he looked up at the shore, and silently thanked his foe for leading them to a beautiful new home.

Mission over, Kupe weighed anchor and did some exploring. Then he sailed back to Hawaiki. But he knew his mokopuna would return one day to Aotearoa, the land of the long white cloud.

Glossary

āe yes, to agree

ao world

Aotearoa 'land of the long white cloud', New Zealand

arero carved point of a taiaha

atua deity

auē expression of astonishment

awa river

e hē! no way!

e hoa mā friend, my friend

haere ki te pō, e hoa depart into the night, my friend

haere mai come here, welcome

haere mai ki tōku whare come to my house

haerenga journey

harakeke New Zealand flax used in weaving

hau tonga southerly wind

Hawaiki celestial realm, origin of Māori

hei tiki pendant shaped like a human

hoa friend, companion, ally

hoariri opponent, enemy

hoe paddle

hōhā annoyed, fed up

hongi press noses in greeting, exchange of breath

hui meeting

huru feather

ika fish

Io supreme being

iwi group of people descended from a common ancestor

ka kite anō au i a koe I'll see you again

kāhu harrier hawk

kahu huruhuru feather cloak

kahu kiwi kiwi feather cloak

kai food

kāinga home

kaipuke ship

kaitaka fine cloak

kākahu cloak

kāniwha barb of a fish hook

karakia prayer

kārearea New Zealand falcon

kawau cormorant, shag

kete woven bag

kōauau flute

kōhanga nest, nursery

kōkōwai red pigment

korowai a type of cloak

kōwhaiwhai painted ornamentation

kuia female elder

mana power, authority, prestige

manu bird

marae an open area around the wharenui

matau fish hook

maunga mountain

mere a short flat greenstone weapon

mīharo amazing, astonishing

moana ocean

mokopuna grandchild

muka flax fibre

ngahere forest

nui important, large

pā fortified village

pakanga battle

Pākehā New Zealander of European descent

Glossary (continued)

pekapeka bat

pepeke insect

pīpīwharauroa shining cuckoo

pītau fern shoot, spiral shape

pōtaka spinning top

pounamu greenstone, New Zealand jade

poupou carved panels

poutama a stepped pattern

puhi woman of high rank

pūtātara conch shell trumpet

rā sun

rākau tree

rangatira chief, noble

raupō bulrush

repo swamp

taiaha long wooden weapon

tāne man, male

tangi mourn, cry

taniwha fire spirits

taonga cultural treasure

taonga puoro musical instrument

tapu sacred, restricted

tauihu waka prow

Te Moana-nui-a-Kiwa Pacific Ocean

tinana body, trunk

tītī muttonbird

titiro look at, inspect

toa red-brown dye

tohunga priest, seer

toki adze, axe

toroa albatross

tuna eel

upoko head

waeroa mosquito

wahine toa warrior woman

wai water

waiata song

waka canoe

waka taua war canoe

wānanga school of knowledge

wero challenge, friend or foe

whakairo pattern

whakaora rescue, heal

whakarongo listen

whakatau decide

whānau family

whare house

wharekura house of learning, school

whatukura sacred stones of knowledge

wharenui meeting house

whawhai fight, quarrel

wheke octopus

whenua land

About the taonga

Ko Tāne me ngā Kete o te Wānanga
Tāne and the Kete of Knowledge
Kete whakairo
(1800–33)
Unknown maker
Harakeke
Te Papa (ME013967), purchased 1977

Ko te Kaitaka Whakaora o Ruhia
Ruhia's Life-saving Cloak
Kaitaka paepaeroa
(1800–40)
Unknown maker
Muka, bark, dye
Te Papa (DE000107/1)

Te Tūtakinga Kino o te tau 1769
The Deadly Encounter of 1769
Hoe (1700–70)
Unknown maker
Wood, pāua, paint
Te Papa (ME014921), purchased 1987
with New Zealand Lottery Board funds

Ko te Pakanga a ngā Manu
Battle of the Birds
Kahu huruhuru
Unknown maker
Muka, feather, wool
Te Papa (ME014165), purchased 1979

Ko te Whakatau Nui a Willie Apiata
Willie Apiata and the Tough Decision
Desert Disruptive Pattern Material uniform
(about 2000)
New Zealand Defence Force and Whitehead
Productions
Cotton, polyester, plastic, metal
Te Papa (GH017487), gift of Corporal BH
Apiata, VC, 2012

Ko Hēni me te Pakanga ki Pukehinahina
Hēni and the Battle of Gate Pā
Letter to WF Gordon (16 March 1900)
Hēni Te Kiri Karamu
Paper, ink
Te Papa (CA000162/001/0010/0005)

Ko Rata me ngā Tamariki a Tāne
Rata and the Children of Tāne
Tauihu (1880s)
Unknown maker
Wood, pāua
Te Papa (ME010929)

Te Whawhai i te Repo
The Battle in the Swamp
Taiaha
(1800–63)
Unknown maker
Wood, pāua
Te Papa (WE000008), bequest of
Kenneth Athol Webster, 1971

Kua Mau i te Hau Tonga
Seized by the Cold South Wind
Stone
Volcanic rock
Te Papa (ME014411), purchased 1984

Ko Tarakiuta rāua ko Tarakitai
The Tale of Tarakiuta and Tarakitai
Pōtaka
Unknown maker
Wood, pāua
Te Papa (ME001502), purchased early
1900s

Ko Hinemoa rāua ko Tūtānekai
Hinemoa and Tūtānekai
Kōauau
Unknown maker
Bone
Te Papa (ME003932)

Ko te *Kaipuke Karihi-Kore*
The *Rainbow Warrior*
'French Letter'
(1982)
Herbs, Warrior Records
Paper, vinyl
Te Papa (GH009830), purchased 2001

Ko Māui me te Ika Nunui
Māui and the Big Catch
Matau
Unknown maker
Bone
Te Papa (ME023242), purchased 2003

Ko Huria me te Kaipuke
Huria and the Shipwreck
Korowai (about 1870)
Matenga Huria
Harakeke, muka, wool
Te Papa (ME023290), purchased
2004

Te Paea me te Waka Wairua
Te Paea and the Ghost Waka
Sophia's whare, Wairoa, after eruption,
(10 June 1886)
Frederick Muir for the Burton Brothers
Studio
Black and white gelatin glass negative
Te Papa (C.010327), purchased 1943

Te Kauranga Nui a Kahe
Kahe's Epic Swim
Hei tiki (1800s)
Tangiwai
Private collection

Te Ngarohanga o ngā Parirau o te Kiwi
How the Kiwi Lost Its Wings
Kahu kiwi (1850–1900)
Unknown maker
Muka, feathers, dye
Te Papa (ME002701), gift of Alexander
Turnbull, 1913

Ko Kupe me te Wheke Nunui
Kupe and the Giant Wheke
Punga
Unknown maker
Greywacke
Te Papa (ME015920)

About the artists

Reweti Arapere (Ngāti Raukawa, Ngāti Porou and Ngāti Tūwharetoa) holds a Master of Māori Visual Arts from Toioho ki Apiti School of Māori Studies, Massey University, and has exhibited extensively both throughout Aotearoa New Zealand and internationally. His art practice is contextualised through drawing and he is committed to representing customary Māori narratives in a contemporary light.

Ariki Brightwell (Te Whānau-a-Ruataupere, Rongowhakaata, Ngāti Kahungunu ki Heretaunga, Ngāti Mutunga, Rangitāne, Ngāti Raukawa, Te Arawa ki Tūwharetoa, Tahiti, Ra'iātea, Rarotonga) was born in 1989 in Tūranga-nui-a-Kiwa (Gisborne) and lives in Te Whanganui-a-Tara (Wellington). She graduated from Massey University in 2013 with a Bachelor of Video Communications Design and works at Te Wharewaka o Poneke and as a freelance artist. Ariki says: 'I am an indigenous artist of Māori and Tahitian descent. I spent my entire life practising the arts; it's in my blood. I gather much of my influence in Te Ao Māori from my father Matahi Brightwell, a tohunga whakairo (master carver) who is one of the most renowned Māori artists in Aotearoa.

Another medium that inspired my art was eastern/western cartoons and the pop culture I grew up with in the 1990s and early 2000s. The aim of my art is to tell our stories and the whakapapa of the land as our ancestors did. I produce this in the forms of murals, paintings and digital works by incorporating both modern and traditional styles. Being part of this project was a dream come true. I am proud of my heritage and it is an honour to draw our history and the stories of our tipuna.'

Te Hana Goodyer (Ngāti Raukawa ki te Tonga) graduated from Massey University in 2016. He lives in London, where he works as a product designer for an ecommerce tech start-up. He is an experienced user interface designer who also works as a freelance digital illustrator and animator. Te Hana's areas of focus are kaupapa Māori, hip hop and anime. 'They are my sources of inspiration and influence, which motivate me in my everyday life.'

Miriama Grace-Smith (Ngāti Hau, Ngāti Maniapoto, Ngāti Toa and Ngāti Porou) has been creating art for most of her life. Her preferred mediums are painting, printmaking, tā moko, illustration and fashion design. Miriama completed a

Certificate in Visual Arts at Whitireia Polytechnic and went on to graduate with a Bachelor of Fine Arts from Massey University. Miriama's education in the arts encouraged her to pursue a career doing what she loves – making art. Much of her work depicts traditional village life, explores natural phenomena and draws from pūrākau Māori. Miriama is a member of Māori women's art collective Hine Pae Kura, and has her own streetwear label Foresight Clothing.

Isobel Joy Te Aho-White
(Ngāti Kahungunu ki Te Wairoa, Rongomaiwahine, Ngāi Tahu, Ngāti Irakehu) is a graphic artist with a diploma in Visual Arts (UCOL) and a Bachelor of Design (Hons) majoring in illustration from Massey University. Izzy was born in 1988 and grew up in Te Whanganui-a-Tara (Wellington) and the Wairarapa, where her parents passed on to her a keen interest in native plants and birdlife. Her work explores themes of mana wāhine/the sacred feminine, kaitiakitanga, nature and darkness, while her artistic inspirations come from an eclectic combination of artists and illustrators, old and new. Izzy lives in Wellington, where she freelances as an illustrator in a variety of mediums, both digital and traditional.

Huriana Kopeke-Te Aho is a
self-taught freelance artist of Ngāi Tūhoe, Ngāti Porou, Rongowhakaata, Te Āti Haunui-a-Pāpārangi, Ngāi Tahu and Ngāti Kahungunu descent based in Tāmaki Makaurau/Auckland.

They also whakapapa to Sāmoa, Tahiti, Ireland, Scotland and Denmark. They have worked with the University of Waikato, Auckland Pride, The Wireless, Ara Taiohi, Pantograph Punch and Gender Minorities Aotearoa, amongst others.

Josh Morgan (Te Aitanga-a-Māhaki, Rongowhaakata) is a
picture book illustrator who lives in Wellington with his family and a vast hoard of picture books. His digital illustrations are created to evoke the charm and quirkiness of the classic picture books and animations he grew up with (and still loves). He is very proud that many of his projects, including the award-winning picture books he has produced with writer Sacha Cotter, have been from a Māori perspective. He also considers himself very fortunate to have worked on this project, especially sharing a story from his ancestral rohe.

Munro Te Whata (Ngā Puhi, Ngāti Porou) is Māori Niuean and is
from South Auckland. He began drawing at a very young age with his cousins. After dropping out of high school (because all he did was draw) he found animation school. He was trained in traditional paper animation and later worked on *Bro'town* as an animator. He then worked at Māori TV and that led to him giving up on animation. After a year of travel he decided to get a degree in creative writing and he also started getting illustrating work, which he has been doing ever since.

Acknowledgements

This book is based on the web series *He Paki Taonga i a Māui*. Thanks to David Brechin-Smith and Ranea Aperahama, who developed the series; to Yvonne Mackay and Production Shed.TV, and Te Wuruhi | Lean Dog, who made the series; to Kahukura Royal, who plays Māui in the series; to Larry Parr and Te Māngai Pāho; to the illustrators: Munro te Whata (Ngā Puhi, Ngāti Porou, Niue), Te Hana Goodyer (Ngāti Raukawa ki te Tonga), Isobel Joy Te Aho-White (Ngāti Kahungunu ki Te Wairoa, Rongomaiwahine, Ngāi Tahu, Ngāti Irakehu), Ariki Brightwell (Te Whānau-a-Ruataupere, Rongowhakaata, Ngāti Kahungunu ki Heretaunga, Ngāti Mutunga, Rangitāne, Ngāti Raukawa, Te Arawa ki Tūwharetoa, Tahiti, Ra'iātea, Rarotonga), Josh Morgan (Te Aitanga-a-Māhaki, Rongowhaakata), Miriama Grace-Smith (Ngāti Hau, Ngāti Maniapoto, Ngāti Toa, Ngāti Porou), Huriana Kopeke-Te Aho (Ngāi Tūhoe, Ngāti Porou, Rongowhakaata, Te Āti Haunui-a-Pāpārangi, Ngāti Kahungunu, Ngāi Tahu), and Reweti Arapere (Ngāti Raukawa, Ngāti Porou, Ngāti Tūwharetoa); to the writers: Matthew Grainger, Victoria Cleal, Jen Craddock and Frances Samuel; to Stephanie Tibble for her Māori language adaptations and translations; to Bo Moore for the web series animations based on the illustrations in this book; to the Te Papa staff who helped in making the series: Matiu Baker, Courtney Johnston, Moana Parata, Puawai Cairns, Anne Peranteau, Sara Guthrie, Anita Schrafft, Jennifer Cauchi, Jennifer Twist, Michael O'Neill, Mark Sykes, Frith Williams, Stephanie Gibson, Nirmala Balram, Dougal Austin, Simon Whittaker, Jason Yorston, Andrew Bruce, Jessica Griffin, Aidy Sanders and Dale Bailey; to the Pātaka staff involved in making the series: Reuben Friend, Kawika Aipa, Laureen Sadlier; to iwi, hapū and whānau who generously supported the use of their stories and taonga in the series and book: Te Āti Awa, Ngāti Tama, Ngāti Toa Rangatira, Ngāti Koata, Ngāti Hāmua/ Te Matehou, Te Arawa, Ngā Koromatua o Ngāti Whakaue, Ngāti Uenuku-Kōpako, Ngāti Hinepare, Ngāti Tūwharetoa, Ngāti Ruanui, Te Aitanga-a-Māhaki Trust, Rongowhakaata Iwi Trust, Ngāti Porou; to all those who helped us get support to share the stories, including: Donna Hall, Melanie McGregor, Taku Parai, Jen Pewhairangi, Paraone Pirika, David Pitt, Miria Pomare, Manutai Schuster, Hemi Sundgren, Nuki Takao, Hone Nuku Tarawhiti, Jamie Tuuta, Chris Winitana, Jodie Wyllie and Pete Willcox; to Taharakau Stewart and April Nepia-Su'a for their support; to designers Jodi Wicksteed and Liz Tui Morris of Bolster Design; and to Nicola Legat and Claire Gibb at Te Papa Press.

First published in New Zealand in 2019 by
Te Papa Press, PO Box 467, Wellington, New Zealand
www.tepapapress.co.nz

TE PAPA® is the trademark of the Museum of New Zealand Te Papa Tongarewa
Te Papa Press is an imprint of the Museum of New Zealand Te Papa Tongarewa

A catalogue record is available from the National Library of New Zealand

Design by Jodi Wicksteed/Bolster Design
Cover artwork by Munro Te Whata

Series and book based on a concept by David Brechin-Smith

Printed in China by Everbest Printing Co Ltd, China

ISBN 978-0-9951136-2-6